Aunt Mary's Scrapbook

To Vail

Susan Whitford
and Sue Whitford

Aunt Mary's Scrapbook

by
Sue Trammell Whitfield

Photography by Susan T. Whitfield

With
Ann Dunphy Becker

Texasbooks.net
2014

Published by Ann Dunphy Becker

ABCDE
First Printing

Acknowledgements.

To Fay Young Morton, known to her grandchildren as "Mammam", the guiding force at the head of her family. To my father Wash Bryan 'Tex' Trammell, who kept many remnants of his sister's life close to his heart, and whose dedication to his family was unsurpassed by their dedication to him. To my precious children Susan, Bill, Celia, and Trammell. To Ann Dunphy Becker for her encouragement and assistance. To Jay and Laura Moore, Martha Ferguson ,Jeremy Maynard and Stan Trammell for their friendship, research assistance, and hospitality.

Table of Contents

Chapter One – *Introduction*   Page 7

Chapter Two - *Early Years*   Page 17

Chapter Three - *Central High School*   Page 53

Chapter Four - *The Rice Institute*   Page 79

Chapter Five - *Travel and Family*   Page 101

Chapter Six – *West Texas Memories*   Page 127

Mary Jane, Fay Young and Wash Bryan 'Tex' Trammell c. 1910.

Mary Jane Trammell age 7.

Dear Loved Ones,

What follows is a scrapbook assembled by my Aunt Mary almost one hundred years ago. I have always considered it a precious legacy to our family and thus my duty to publish it. I have preserved it for fifty years with the hope that one day I would be able to share it with you. Perhaps it will have some value to those outside my family who wish to see a snapshot of the challenges, beauty, and accomplishments of the Texans of my aunt's generation.

It is my hope that by the end of this scrapbook, you will have some idea of the spirited, brilliant, and independent woman who was my Aunt Mary Jane Trammell. A few of you had the fortune to know her before she passed in 1968. She was born in 1903, two years after my father. The life she packed into her sixty-five years was exciting, patriotic, and giving.

My brothers Bryan, Tom, and I could not wait for her to visit Houston. We looked forward to our month-long vacations in Abilene and at the Y6 Ranch in Hamlin. When our parents would go to their room, we would look to Aunt Mary and say "Please don't go to bed, stay with us and tell us stories." She was so funny! There was never a better story-churner than Aunt Mary. She made us howl with laughter and cringe in fear with the same tale. How I wish there were some recordings of these marvelous stories to share with you. That brain cancer would go on to affect her speech was a painful turn of fate. A lively storyteller was silenced but the woman I loved so much will never be forgotten. For now, enjoy this peek into her history, the world of Aunt Mary.

Mama Sue

This map shows cities where my ancestors lived, loved, died and are buried. In the late 1890's, a handsome, young Walter Trammell would ride his horse the forty-one miles from Sweetwater to Abilene to woo my grandmother Fay "Mammam" Young.

In the early 1900's, my great-grandparents Sam and Julia Young would make the same trip by buggy to visit their two grandchildren, Wash Bryan "Tex" and Mary Jane Trammell.

When my grandfather, Walter Trammell died, it took my parents six hours to drive from Houston to Sweetwater for his funeral. When my grandmother Fay took ill, it was a twelve hour round trip car ride for my father as he picked her up in Abilene to bring her to doctors in Houston.

My family has traversed these roads by horse, buggy and automobile for the past one hundred eighty years. This arid of West Texas land is much part of who we are today and will always mean a great deal to me.

Hamlin

•Abilene

Dallas

Sweetwater

Houston

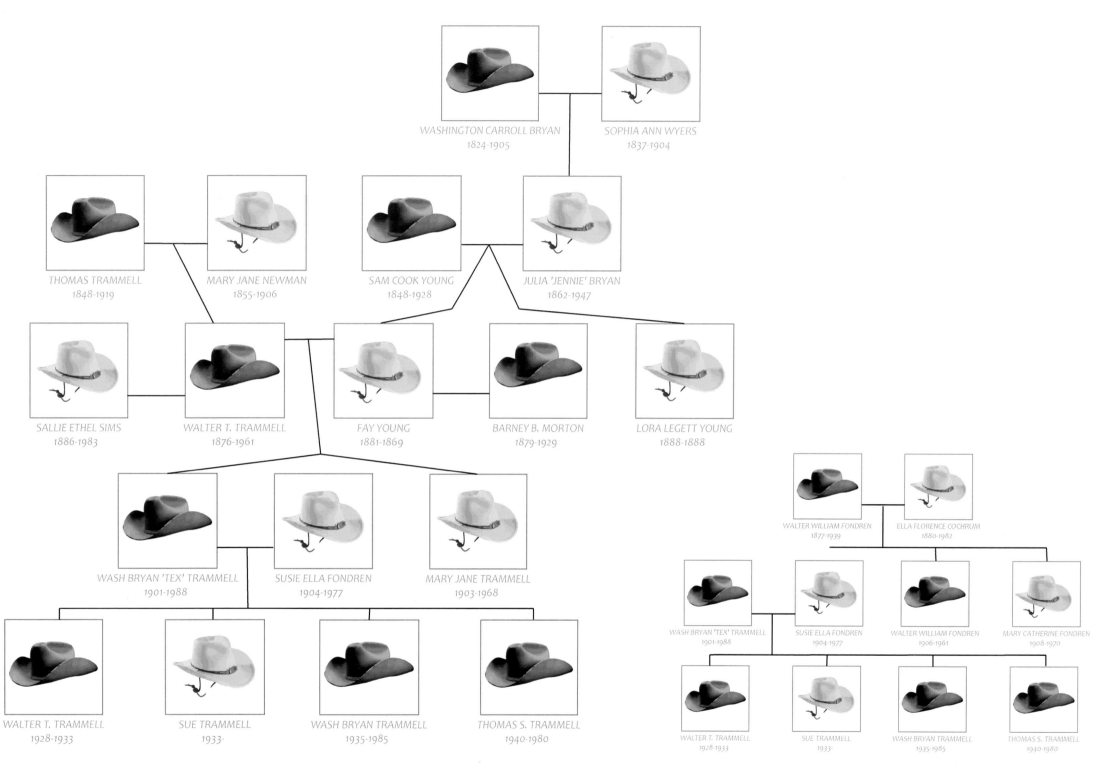

WASHINGTON CARROLL BRYAN
1824-1905

SOPHIA ANN WYERS
1837-1904

THOMAS TRAMMELL
1848-1919

MARY JANE NEWMAN
1855-1906

SAM COOK YOUNG
1848-1928

JULIA 'JENNIE' BRYAN
1862-1947

SALLIE ETHEL SIMS
1886-1983

WALTER T. TRAMMELL
1876-1961

FAY YOUNG
1881-1869

BARNEY B. MORTON
1879-1929

LORA LEGETT YOUNG
1888-1888

WASH BRYAN 'TEX' TRAMMELL
1901-1988

SUSIE ELLA FONDREN
1904-1977

MARY JANE TRAMMELL
1903-1968

WALTER T. TRAMMELL
1928-1933

SUE TRAMMELL
1933-

WASH BRYAN TRAMMELL
1935-1985

THOMAS S. TRAMMELL
1940-1980

WALTER WILLIAM FONDREN
1877-1939

ELLA FLORENCE COCHRUM
1880-1982

WASH BRYAN 'TEX' TRAMMELL
1901-1988

SUSIE ELLA FONDREN
1904-1977

WALTER WILLIAM FONDREN
1906-1961

MARY CATHERINE FONDREN
1908-1970

WALTER T. TRAMMELL
1928-1933

SUE TRAMMELL
1933-

WASH BRYAN TRAMMELL
1935-1985

THOMAS S. TRAMMELL
1940-1980

Trammell, Newman, Bryan, Wyres, Young

Fondren, Cochrum, Trammell

The town of Sweetwater where Thomas and Mary Jane Trammell walked the dusty streets and, planted mesquite, juniper and oak saplings. They also raised three boisterous sons, opened the first bank in 1881 and by 1883, they helped bring the railroad through Texas on the way to the west coast.

1888

The Trammell Bank opened in 1883 and is the two story building pictured on the far right.

Mary Jane Trammell age 13.

Mary Jane Trammell was born in Sweetwater, Texas on May 13, 1903. She was Walter and Fay's only daughter, following her brother Wash Bryan "Tex" by two years. From racing across the flatlands on horseback to shooting copperheads, Mary had a unique upbringing worthy of a Hollywood Western.

Trammell men were tough, early pioneers of West Texas, making their living as stockmen and ranchers. Mary Jane's grandfather Thomas Trammell arrived in Sweetwater when it was little more than a tent town. Within a few years, wary of the hazards of mixing alcohol with finances, he opened Sweetwater's first bank in 1883. Prior to this, high finance was conducted in saloons that dotted Sweetwater, often a deadly combination. Trammell's bank and interest in education and railway expansion brought a semblance of controlled growth to the population.

Trammell women had the same determination as their men, but also brought grace and beauty to Sweetwater and Abilene. Photographs, newspaper reports, and archived personal effects paint refined pictures of Mary Jane Newman, Sophia Wyres Bryan, Julie "Jennie" Young, and Fay Young Trammell. On a 2014 research trip to Sweetwater with my daughter Susan, Stan Trammell, and writer Ann Dunphy Becker, I visited the Pioneer City County Museum. The director, Melonnie Hicks, brought us a dress once owned by my great-grandmother Mary Jane Newman Trammell. My cousin Stan had donated it to the museum archives. A century later this silk day dress was still lovely, with a fitted bodice and a velvet ribbon trim. Mary Jane lived in a town with dusty, unpaved streets, but she always preferred elegant tailoring. In her sumptuous two-story home, she held parties and served guests on French china. Her daughter-in-law Fay Young was just as feminine and particular about her surroundings. Before her marriage to Walter Thomas Trammell in 1897, Fay was crowned Queen of Love and Beauty at the West Texas Fair.

The men and women of the Trammell clan were polar opposites, but Mary's maternal ancestors were neither weak nor vulnerable. The chemise blouses, sashes, and crinoline slips never hid the Texas iron underneath. My great-great-grandmother Sophia Wyres Bryan, according to Vernon Spence, author of *Pioneer Women of Abilene*, was as capable as any man.

"Sophia managed both home and ranch while her husband served in the Confederate Army. ... As a child Sophia tended her younger brothers and sisters, milked cows, tended gardens, fed chickens, cooked meals, and cleaned the house. ... She was an energetic, self-sufficient, and independent woman who was entirely able to care for herself, her children, and the T-Diamond ranch during her husband's absences. ... (Sophia) could shoot straight, cut cattle and snap a snake's head with the flop of her wrist. ... When in public view, Sophia dressed well, with layers and layers of petticoats."

My grandparents, Walter and Fay Young Trammell, had two fine children. For reasons not yet found in any hidden diary or letters, the Trammells separated when Mary was about eight. Fay and Mary left Sweetwater and traveled between Dallas, Houston, and Abilene. They stayed with or near different relatives including the Legett and Jones branches of the family. Meanwhile, Tex remained with his father and the cowboys. Stan Trammell said of his Aunt Mary, *"She wasn't happy when Tex got to stay with Walter. She wanted to be on the ranch too."*

Four generations of West Texas family members. Standing left is Fay Young Trammell "The Queen of Love and Beauty," Right-her mother, Julia "Jennie" Bryan Young. Seated is Julia's mother Sophia Wyers Bryan holding great-grandson Wash Bryan "Tex" Trammell. This picture was taken in 1901.

Though the Trammells had parted ways, both found love in the coming years. In 1913 Walter married Sallie Ethel Sims, a rancher's daughter and the future grandmother of Stan Trammell. Four years later she had a son, Frank Phillip, Tex and Mary's new stepbrother. My grandfather Walter stayed in the ranching business his entire life, married to a woman equally interested in horseflesh and comfortable with the sunup-to-sundown routine. This life fulfilled him to his last days. Walter loved raising horses. Known throughout Texas for their speed, his horses would go on to influence today's American Quarter Horse. Shue Fly, an eminent racehorse of the 1940s, could trace a bloodline back to Sweetwater and the Trammell Ranch. *The Abilene Reporter News* on February 18, 1945, quoted Walter Trammell as saying *"a stallion should never be used until it is known if he can handle."* My grandfather had strong horse sense and took great care in training his prized stallions. One of which he named Walter Trammell.

Rice Hotel Photograph c. 1920

In 1915, Fay Young Trammell married Barney B. Morton, a successful hotelier. Her life took an exciting new turn as she went from the West Texas plains to the Hotel Galvez in Galveston and eventually to the Rice Hotel, where her new husband was the manager. It was the perfect lifestyle for her. The luxuriously elegant interiors, fine cuisine, lavish parties, and frequent bridge tournaments keenly suited Fay's taste for refined opulence. Well respected in his field, Barney was elected president of the Texas Hotel Keepers Association in 1924. At times both my father Tex and Aunt Mary are listed as residents of the Rice Hotel, and it was the scene of many of our more significant family events.

Mary and her mother Fay were smart, strong, and independent, but embodied different generations—the fading of one century and the infancy of the next. Fay came from the elegant Victorian Era and Mary lived in the spirited Flapper Age. Fay wore silk and lace dresses, petticoats, and button-up shoes; Mary preferred slacks and the more masculine fashions of the day. Mary was seventeen when suffragists landed women the right to vote in 1920. It is not surprising that her scrapbook has pictures of young women dressed in masculine attire and dress ties. The era of equal rights had just begun and that included style of dress. In 1917, Mary was enrolled in the Hockaday School for Girls in Dallas while Tex was attended to the Culver Military Academy in Indiana. There is only speculation why Fay and Walter chose these private schools, but their choices shaped two very independent, thoughtful, and articulate young adults.

Houston's Welcome to the World

A house that combines pleasing service with genuine hospitality

*Complete in all
respects including
unexcelled Cafe,
quick Lunch Room,
Turkish Baths
and
Swimming Pool,
Barber Shop, etc.*

*During the summer
months meals
served on Rice
Roof Garden,
eighteen stores up
above the heat,
dust and noise of
the busy street.*

THE RICE

B. B. Morton, Mgr.   Houston, Texas

This picture is an example of B.B. Morton's knack for promoting his "unexcelled" hotel amenities.

Tex graduated from Culver and enrolled in the University of Texas at Austin. Mary attended Hockaday, Kent Place School in Summit, New Jersey, and Central High School in Houston. She went on to attend the Rice Institute. A story I heard many times was,

Aunt Mary had broken her leg while at boarding school. She and several friends crawled out onto the roof of a building to shoot pictures. They looked out and were horrified to see a teacher walking down below who spotted them. Her friends scampered back into the building, but Mary because of her cast was slower and was spotted on the roof. That was the end of her attendance at that particular school.

Mary Jane's scrapbook takes readers through the doors of Hockaday School for Girls, Kent Place School, and Central High School. Mary journeyed with friends through Yellowstone National Park, Stapp's Lake, Wyoming, and Colorado. The following pages are filled with many friends, scenic destinations and early automobiles. These candid photographs capture the smiles and laughter of everyday student life. This was Mary Jane Trammell's world between the ages of 14 and 22

One original scrapbook has a black leather cover. Inside, beneath the photographs, Aunt Mary used a white pen to write the descriptions. The image below is the book's first message. Notice the slight forward slant to the script, the evenness of the spacing, and the capitalized letters. In graphology, this penmanship might indicate an outgoing, strong yet humble individual who dances to her own music. Many wonderful dedications were made to her from fellow students and faculty.

Aunt Mary was a unique, funny, giving and smart woman. I like to say that God broke the mold when she was created. Everyone who knew her had the same response when I mentioned putting this book together. Their sentiment was, "I loved Aunt Mary!" I hope you enjoy this walk through time as much as we enjoyed producing it.

Directly from the scrapbook this penmanship demonstrates Mary's healthy sense of self.

Chapter 2

Early Years

Aunt Mary at sixteen.

The Trammell-Young marriage ended around 1910. Aunt Mary left with my grandmother, while my father Tex stayed in Sweetwater with Walter. During the first ten years of their lives, Tex and Mary attended a one-room schoolhouse in Sweetwater. After their parents' separation, the teenage siblings went away to school. Tex was enrolled in the Culver Military Academy in Indiana and Mary was sent to the Hockaday School for Girls in Dallas.

The Hockaday School was founded by a talented young teacher named Ela Hockaday. She was asked by multiple Dallas families to consider creating a school that would prepare young women for college and life in general. She accepted the challenge and opened the school in 1913. With her refined manners and exquisite taste, one might say Ela was properly bred in the traditional ways of a 19th-century woman. Designing an educational system for the 20th-century woman was a feat through which she rose to acclaim. Her efforts and successes are still evident on the Dallas campus today. In 1941, the *Christian Science Monitor* noted, *"Miss Ela Hockaday has accomplished the so-called impossible. She has made a private school pay its own way, not endowed or tax supported. Today she is president and active head of a school with a student body that numbers 450, a staff of 83, and a plant approaching a million dollars in value, still not endowed, still the complete servant of its president."*

Students who attended the school came from varied backgrounds and lifestyles. Aunt Mary had spent the first decade of her life caring for horses, hanging around rugged cowboys, and running the dusty streets of Sweetwater. Apart from the occasional party dress given by her mother, Mary's wardrobe was made up of boots and slacks. And, according to nephew Stan Trammell, that suited Mary just fine. In family lore, Fay wanted to groom her daughter into the type of young lady she herself was. Fay was a refined, polished woman. She believed an environment where manners, academics, and sports were instilled by a woman of Ela Hockaday's caliber would rein in her roughshod daughter. Thus at age fourteen Mary entered the structured world of Ela Hockaday.

Mary's scrapbook indicates she had a great time at Hockaday, even with a stricter hand in charge. Brave, curious, and quick to smile, she made fast friends, including Miss Hockaday's own niece Ruth Kerr Johnson. The scrapbook begins with photographs from her 1917- 1921 school years and gives some wonderful snapshots of the Granville Campus. By 1917, the four-year-old school had grown to around a hundred students. Many of these young women left inside jokes and amusing comments on photographs in her scrapbook.

Ruth Kerr Johnson

The first page in the scrapbook opens to the smiling face of Mary's best school friend, Ruth Kerr Johnson, the founder's niece.

Hockaday's first school located in a house on North Haskell Avenue in Dallas.

Ela was a graduate of teachers' college in Denton. On the recommendation of headmaster M. B. Terrill, a group of Dallas residents invited her to establish a girls preparatory school that would be the equivalent of the boys school Terrill was operating. She hired her teaching colleague and friend Sarah Trent as faculty, and on September 25, 1913, she opened the doors of the school. She had ten students and faculty of five and she served as president of the Hockaday School for Girls. The picture to the left was taken in 1917.

The first curriculum included mathematics, history, Latin, English, French, and German. Notice Mary Jane Trammell sitting far left and Ela Hockaday in the middle of the photo. Mary left Hockaday in 1921. The first scrapbook chronicles wonderful friendships and activities during her teen and college years across several schools.

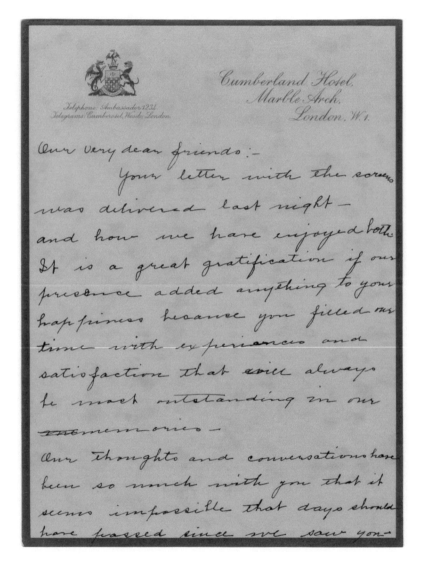

Ela Hockaday and Gertrude Stein continued to correspond for many years after meeting in early 1900.

Ms. Hockaday and her friends were truly women before their time. Their plans for progressive education is still in use today such as the importance of physical education and college preparation.

THE HOCKADAY SCHOOL
INCORPORATED
DALLAS, TEXAS

January 11, 1937

My dear Miss Stein,

How can I thank you and Miss Toklas for the thrill you gave my travellers? It was indeed kind of you to entertain so graciously such a bevy of girls. They have written most enthusiastic descriptions of what is easily the high light of the trip. It was really a coal of fire on my head for I am aware that I have been a most negligent correspondent. My friends are probably to blame for they have been too indulgent towards this fault of mine.

Early in the season I learned from our newspapers that you were planning another visit to our country and that, of course, means Texas. Your tiny suite at "The Cottage" is yearning for your coming and so are all of us. Exie has learned to make some new dishes that I am sure will appeal to you both. We have made some additions I want to show you, a new residence for Sophomores, and have doubled the size of our dining room, all warranted by our increased enrollment. The good times seen at last to be coming around the corner.

We are thrilled beyond words over a letter from Mr. Louis Bromfield asking for information about the school, this at your instigation and for which we are most grateful to you. We immediately sent our catalogues and pictures to him and sincerely hope that we shall have the pleasure of enrolling his three little daughters.

As I sit and look out my window over the campus I can well imagine that I am in the cold and icy north. The ground is white with snow and every tree and twig is covered in a heavy coat of ice. It is a most gorgeous sight, a veritable fairy land, though the trees are groaning under their heavy load, some of them bending over to touch the ground and many limbs being broken off completely. This wintry weather has lasted for five days and is such a novelty for us that the girls are having the thrill of their lives.

Again, thank you many times for your gracious hospitality to my travelling family. Miss Morgan and I both send our best wishes to you and Miss Toklas and shall look forward to seeing you in Texas before the winter is gone.

Your very sincere friend,

Ela Hockaday

EH:j

Miss Gertrude Stein
Paris, France

Straight from the Dallas-Fort Worth area and her father's home in Sweetwater, young Aunt Mary was soon immersed in Miss Hockaday's vision. The headmistress believed in a four-sided foundation comprised of character, courtesy, scholarship, and athletics. She also acutely understood the evolving role of women in American society. Among visitors to the school were Eleanor Roosevelt and Gertrude Stein, proponents of women's rights.

Alice Toklas, wrote about their visit in The *Alice B. Toklas Cookbook*:

"On to Dallas where we went to stay with Miss Ela Hockaday at her Junior College. It was a fresh new world. Gertrude Stein became attached to the young students, to Miss Hockaday, and the life in Miss Hockaday's home and on the campus ... The only recipe I carried away was for corn sticks, not knowing in my ignorance that a special iron was required in which to bake them. But when we sailed back to France in my stateroom one was waiting for me, a proof of Miss Hockaday's continuing attentiveness."

Gertrude Stein and Alice Toklas were lifelong friends.

Sarah Cash

The Hockaday Athletic Association 1917 - 1918

Agnes Coe

Ruby Thompson

US Boarders

Judy Hunt

In 1919 Residence Program grows to fifty boarders

An advertisement placed in the *Galveston Daily News* on August 13, 1922 describes Hockaday as a *"College Preparatory School which meets the requirements of Wellesley, Vassar, Smith, and other Eastern colleges."* The ad also listed departments and teachers qualifications and concluded with *"The Home Department is headed by Miss Miriam Morgan, a woman of broad experience, quick sympathy, and a wonderful understanding of girls. You will be content to place your daughter under her influence and care."*

Mary Jane Trammell is in the second row from the top, fifth from the right.

"I was mightily impressed with the trappings of this legendary private school. My earliest letters to my parents after I assumed my teaching job recall a headmaster's dinner with standing rib roast, Caesar salad, and crème de menthe pie. A buffet dinner with resident students and their parents whose nametags read like a Texas Who's who was no less sumptuous: chicken Kiev, ham rollups, green rice, plus silver trays of cold shrimp and fresh fruit. Dessert was a fluffy lemon mousse with toasted almonds." Texas writer Prudence MacIntosh

Mary and her brother Tex enjoyed a lively camaraderie whether in Abilene, Houston or on the Y6 Ranch in Hamlin. They spent time with both parents Walter and Fay but rarely, if ever, at the same event.

Her favorite nickname for Tex was "Bud."

Keeping up with Tex propelled Mary toward the success she became. They were rarely idle as youngsters and grew accustomed to new environments and a wealth of unique personalities. The siblings had a great deal in common, in particular a magnetism which drew people to them. If you entered a party and saw a crowd gathered you would find a Trammell at the center.

Wash Bryan "Tex" Trammell (1901-1988)

Mary Jane Trammell (1903-1968)

Aunt Mary's Hockaday Friends.

Audrey Cook

Judy Hunt

Margaret Harris

Mary Payne

Kathleen

Marion and Me

Typical of Aunt Mary's humor are her captions. Audrey Cook is *"The Girl Who Chewed Tobacco"* and her friends are *"That Old Gang of Mine."* My Aunt Mary took many of these photos herself. She must have been standing right in front of Louise Nolan on the donkeys, or artistically stretched out on the ground to take the shot of Ruth and Sidney Grogan (above).

Elizabeth Beeler

Beeler Child

More of Beeler

Elizabeth Beeler, Mary's roommate, signed this picture "Give Me Some, Elizabeth."

"When Miss Hockaday established her school in 1913, she made sure the young women would participate actively and competitively in a wide range of athletics. She felt that participation in athletics would teach the students teamwork and leadership skills. Hockaday girls were taught that whether they won or lost, they should do so with grace, humility and respect for each other and their opponent…A curriculum steeped in both the classics and modern thought was what defined Miss Hockaday's School for Girls. Students studied the classics, learned to appreciate the fine arts and welcomed modern-day thinkers as guest lecturers to the school, such as Gertrude Stein and Alice B. Toklas." Winter 2009 Hockaday Magazine

One of Mary's friends named Gwen was captain of the hockey team. (The picture to the right shows the Hockey team at break). Caption below first picture should be "Gwen"

A – H – Of. A Picture of Stella

Florence Perkins   Ruth   Margaret Martindale   Mary Olive

Birdy and Ruth

Lucy & Ida Nell

There are several pictures of the young woman Mabel Mears. I searched on Ancestry.com and contacted a submitter who seemed to have a good match. It was a great find—Mabel's daughter, Jo Bess Vanderstucken Jackson, shared this story of her mother's Hockaday memories.

Mabel Mears

"Mother and Ethel both attended Hockaday, Mother graduating in about 1924 and Ethel a year or so later. Mother excelled academically and in tennis. She wrote a column for the school newsletter, reporting on her classmates' activities. My impression is that the 'boarders' were in a lower social level than the Dallas day student girls. But for all that, Mother was elected president of the student body (Mabel was a US boarder). Apparently Miss Hockaday was a stern taskmaster and ruled with an iron fist. Once, Mother was upset because Miss Hockaday had degraded and talked down to a girl in front of a crowd of students. It was for some perceived failing or deficiency. Mother just didn't think that was right. And she couldn't let it go. So she made an appointment and actually met with Miss Hockaday—a bold move. Mother told Miss Hockaday that she thought it was wrong and unfair for Miss Hockaday to speak that way to the poor frightened girl, who also was from a small town and a long way from home. I don't know the outcome, but the story says a lot about Mother."

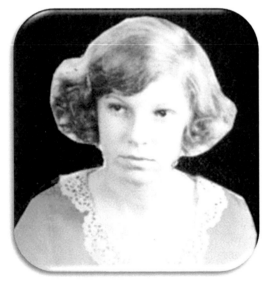

Judy Hunt

Mary Whitwer

Greenville Avenue Campus in 1920.

My 1ˢᵗ Roommate Marion Burrett

Ruth dropped a stitch

Ruth

My Buddy Stella

Lucy, Virginia Bohers, Winnie Baker

Estelle Garner, My Buddy

In 1920, Ruth's camera would have cost $4, which today would equal $80.00.

The Adolphus
DALLAS, TEXAS

DALLAS, TEX.
SEP 16
8.30 AM
JACKSON ST.

1314

Miss Mary Trammell,

% Rice Hotel,

Houston, Texas.

Aunt Mary's stepfather B. B. Morton was a well-known and respected hotelier. Her mother Fay Young Morton was as close to Abilene royalty as possible. It was not surprising that the Texas Centennial Pageant would actively seek Mary's participation. When she did attend this type of event it was more to please my grandmother Fay than her own interest. Aunt Mary was a tomboy at heart.

TEXAS CENTENNIAL PAGEANT
OCTOBER EIGHTH NINETEEN TWENTY ONE
DALLAS

September 8, 1921.

TO YOUR ROYAL HIGHNESS, PRINCESS MARY:

It is with great pleasure that the principality of Dallas summons you to the International Court of Her Majesty, the first Queen of Dallas, to which honor you have been officially appointed, and to witness the Texas Centennial Pageant in her honor, formally opening the State Fair of Texas and International Exposition, Saturday evening, October eighth, nineteen hundred and twenty one, at eight o'clock, and to remain for the Court functions which are to take place in this City for two weeks following.

You are to be attended by a Prince and two Ladies in Waiting, each of whom are to be escorted by Knights, which comprises your Royal Party as should be present to court rehearsal, Friday evening, October seventh, at seven thirty o'clock, in the new Dallas Stadium which the Texas Centennial Pageant will dedicate.

Court regalia is to consist of an evening gown and court train, to be at least three yards in length, with or without Elizabethean collar. Ornamental staffs are to be carried, topped with fans or plumes, harmonizing with your apparel, which may be of any desired colors, trimmed with metallics, sequins, crystals, rhinestones, fringe or other ornamentation. Pearls, flowers, tassels, rhinestones or other decoration may form a shower from the head of your staff. Original and extreme tiaras, or head-dresses, will add much to your magnificence. Escorts are to appear in conventional evening dress.

An information booth, for the pleasure and convenience of the visiting Royalty, will be maintained in the parlor of the Adolphus Hotel. In event you are unable to bring an escort the Court Committee will appoint a Dallas gentleman to that office.

Trusting that you will honor us with photographs of the personnel of your Royal Party, upon your acceptance, and awaiting your reply that we may extend a formal invitation and the courtesies of our City, we remain

Respectfully,

Lunen Jester
Chairman Court Committee.

JackWebster Harkrider

Miss Mary Trammell,
C/o Rice Hotel,
Houston, Texas.

Jack Webster Harkrider,   Suite 415
Pageant Master.   Adolphus Hotel.

The Adolphus

OWNED AND OPERATED BY
THE DALLAS HOTEL COMPANY.

R.B. ELLIFRITZ, MANAGING DIRECTOR

Dallas, Texas

Sept. 15th, 1921.

Miss Mary Trammell,
Princess of Smith School,
Care Rice Hotel,
Houston, Texas.

My dear Princess:

We understand with pleasure that you are to honor the Principality of Dallas with your presence during the Coronation Ceremonies of Her Majesty - Queen of Dallas.

Permit us to extend you our unparalleled services during your royal visit. Our full and competent corps of officers, clerks and attendants will be at your beck and call.

We are exceptionally well located and equipped in every way to make your visit most comfortable and enjoyable while within our domain. Our hotel is the only real fireproof hotel in Dallas and our cuisine is unsurpassed.

In view of the fact that there are to be thousands of people visiting our wonderful Principality during this event, may we not expect an early request from you for accommodations.

Anxiously awaiting your slightest commands and again assuring you of our earnest hope that you will honor us with a visit, we remain, our dear Princess, your obedient servant.

THE ADOLPHUS

R. B. Ellifritz

Managing Director
The Dallas Hotel Company

While conducting research for this volume we were in contact with Emily Embry, the archives manager at Hockaday and received this email correspondence: *"Thank you for your email. Our records indicate that Mary Jane Trammell graduated from The Hockaday School in 1921. Unfortunately, during this time the only two yearbooks were published in 1917 and then in 1923."* Luckily and much to our happiness, Aunt Mary's scrapbook is just as good as any yearbook with the same kind of pictures and personalized comments from her days at Hockaday on the Greenville Avenue campus. Captured in her photographs, scanned and reprinted here, the atmosphere of everyday school life comes alive.

Research on this volume took me, my daughter Susan Whitfield, and Ann Becker on a fun journey. We traveled from Santa Fe, New Mexico, to Abilene, Hamlin, and Sweetwater in Texas. In Abilene, local historian Jay Moore and his wife Laura, director of the Grace Museum, were great resources. Their home in Abilene is the same house that Aunt Mary's grandparents lived in, and she was a frequent visitor. I took this as a gesture from heaven that Aunt Mary's story must be told. She was a giving, wonderful person. While conducting research in Santa Fe, we discovered a slim red volume among her carefully stored effects—a yearbook from the Kent Place School in Summit, New Jersey. This showed Aunt Mary's attendance during her junior year of high school. We discovered more of her friends, and more instances of her athleticism and warmth.

On their website Kent Place School describes their history *"Over 100 years ago in the spring of 1894, a group of Summit, NJ, businessmen and fathers met at an informal dinner to discuss the establishment of a school for girls. They were determined that their daughters would receive an education equal in quality to that which was available for their sons. Their determination would alter the course of education for generations of young women to come. Later that fall, on an estate in the heart of Summit, which was once the summer home of New York State Chancellor James Kent (1763-1847), Kent Place School for Girls opened its doors to a small group of day students. The operation of the entire school was confined to one building, and the tenure of its first principal, Amelia S. Watts, lasted only two years. Nevertheless, the Kent Place vision of fine academic training in a supportive setting was born. When the school opened for its third year, in the fall of 1896, the trustees, then known as shareholders of the Summit School Company, announced the appointment of Mrs. Sarah Woodman Paul as principal of the school, and her sister, Miss Anna Sophia Woodman, as assistant principal. Meanwhile, Kent Place began accepting boarding students, a tradition that was to continue until 1968. Six boarders were among the 18 Lower School and 36 Upper School students enrolled at Kent Place in 1896.*

Girls Use Bible as Their Etiquet Book

(By NEA News Service)
SUMMIT, N. J., June 21—Discovered: A school for girls where the students do not smoke, do not brag, do not get boisterous—a school whose graduates for 27 years have a college record of no dismissals for misconduct and no failures in examinations.

The secret is that a new text-book on etiquet has been found. It is the Bible.

The principals of Kent Place School, Mrs. Sarah Woodman Paul and her sister, Miss Anna Sophia Woodman, disclosed their secret during commencement exercises. It was the twenty-seventh commencement since they became principals of the school two years after it was founded on the estate of the famous Chancellor Kent, America's "Blackstone."

"Grace of manner will solve all the problems of every school girl," they say. "The best way to acquire it is to read the 'charity chapter' of the Bible, the 13th chapter of First Corinthians."

Vogues of modern women and flappers, and even heart-breaking stiffness of examinations at colleges these days, do not have any effect on the old-fashioned ideals of these women principals.

"What better guide to good manners," says Mrs. Paul, "could any girl have than this: 'Charity suffereth long and is kind; seeketh not her own; is not puffed up; doth not behave herself unseemingly'?

"A girl who comes to Kent School does not smoke, not because of any moral issue involved, but because smoking is against the policy of the school; and 'charity doth not behave herself unseemingly.'

"She doesn't get out of sorts and ruffled because 'charity suffereth long and is kind.'

"She is not boisterous and overly aggressive because 'charity seeketh not her own.'

"She doesn't gossip nor talk about herself and her accomplishments because 'charity is not puffed up.'

"All of these things are a part of good manners. Every girl associates her first night at the school with the reading of 'charity chapter.' Later she may learn dancing and all of the other accomplishments. But to the emphasis which the school lays that all good manners emanate from the heart I attribute the excellent record of our girls."

One of Kent's distinguished graduates some years ago was Miss Annabelle Roberts, of Madison, N. J., the first American woman to die in service in the World War.

MRS. SARAH WOODMAN PAUL (LEFT) AND MISS ANNA SOPHIA WOODMAN, PRINCIPALS OF KENT PLACE SCHOOL.

After graduating from Hockaday in 1921, Mary likely spent the summer driving her car, "Little Hupp," from Houston to Abilene and points in between. Her mother Fay lived in the Rice Hotel, where her step father Barney B. Morton was the general manager, and there were constant splendid events to attend. At least one month during the summer, relatives would gather in Hamlin at the Y6 ranch. In the heat of West Texas summer, the family spent time horseback riding, hunting, and picking wild plums. It was an idyllic remembrance of her childhood, but at seventeen, Mary perhaps found the ranch a bit too far from the bustling city. In the Fall of 1922, she attended Kent Place School in Summit, New Jersey.

It was an interim period for Mary. With the undoubted influence of Fay, she was enrolled in a school that was featured by the 1923 NEA News Service as *"A school for girls where the students do not smoke, do not brag, do not get boisterous—a school whose graduates for 2 years have a college record of no dismissal for misconduct and no failures in examinations. The secret is that new textbook etiquet has been found. It is the Bible."* These secrets were disclosed during commencement exercises two years after Mary was in attendance, by the principals Sarah Woodman Paul and her sister Anna Sophia Woodman.

THE · LOG

1921

"And furthermore, my daughters, be admonished; of making many books there is no end; and much study is a weariness of the flesh."
—*Ecclesiastes 12:12.*

KENT PLACE SCHOOL

SUMMIT, NEW JERSEY

Title page in the Kent Place School year book.

Standing in the background, third from left, Aunt Mary appears in the Kent Place School Yearbook as a junior classman.

Kent Place School in 1921 gave kitchen duties to the Junior Class. This was called K.P. or "kitchen patrol". K.P. is a military

term so under the picture of the fire place, in her usual humor Aunt Mary wrote "Where is the Draft?"

Left to Right : Betty and Kay, Kay Westbrook, Sara Jane Porter, Ann (my roommate) and That Cozy K.P. fire.

JUNIOR TEAM

M. Parry (Captain) D. Pillsbury A. Ross E. Day M. Trammel L. Parry M. McCutcheon R. Spencer

Dim Morgan

Gladys Ross

GLADYS ROSS

Summit, N. J.

Six years at Kent Place
Class Treasurer, '19, '20
Treasurer of A. A., '21

Those "Gigglin' Oriental Eyes" tell you loads more about Giddy than we ever could. You needn't take our word for it— just ask West Point! You can't help loving her, even if she does have a bad habit of always being treasurer of something. But there's more to Giddy than her name implies. It would be hard to find another girl with such high ideals of friendship, or one who so well lives up to those ideals.

Bessy Riely

Carrol Hornsey

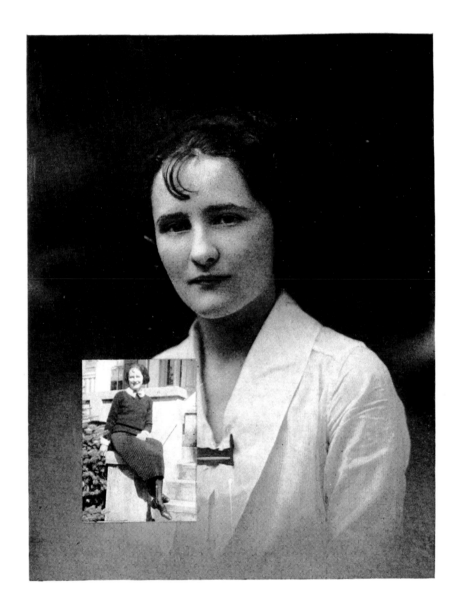

CAROL HORNSEY

Summit, N. J.

Nine years at Kent Place
Basketball, '17, '18, '20, '21

By all rights, Carol's picture ought to be opposite the "pep" chapter—if you knew her as '21 does, you'd never ask why. Anyway, don't you just worship Titian hair? Whether you do or not, if you're a member of '21's basketball team, you've learned that a streak of red is a sure shot in any game. Feeling blue? Go to Kid—which doesn't mean that she'll offer you a sympathetic shoulder to weep upon; she'll just make you realize that there aren't any such things as "blues" in the world.

Chapter 3

Central High School, Houston

1922 *Aegis* Yearbook Page

After completing her junior year of high school on the east coast at Kent Place School, Aunt Mary returned to Houston and lived with her mother and step-father at the Rice Hotel. She spent the summer of 1922 traveling around Texas in her "little hupp" as she fondly referred to her car (left). In 1922 a used Hupmobile sold for $450 which is around $6,000 in 2014 dollars. This model could comfortably hold five passengers and undoubtedly was filled with friends whenever it was driven.

In the fall of 1922, she enrolled in Central High School in Houston. This was located in the heart of downtown Houston, and occupied the entire block of Austin, Capitol, Caroline, and Rusk. This location was one of the oldest sites in Houston to host a school, with the first building erected in 1878. In 1895, Central High was built on the same location and was in use by Houstonians until it burned to the ground in 1919. It is thought that a chemistry project may have been the origin of the fire.

On March 20, 1919 The *Galveston Daily News* reported the *"Central High pupils to attend south end. Estimated loss from fire destroying Houston high school $187.000. Insurance $123,750. The student's records including student's credits and their reports for earlier years were protected in a safe which withstood the fire. The worst loss was the textbooks and the building. Even so, the school board decided to 'weather through' the remainder of the year. In order to continue, the school board decided to replace some equipment such as the chemistry labs."*

Piecing together Aunt Mary's life from scrapbooks, graduate memory books, photographs, letters, and living relatives' accounts has been a challenging but rewarding journey. Her schooling was varied starting with Hockaday in Dallas, moving to Summit, New Jersey, and then to the Houston, all within three years. The scrapbook with which we began our research had little to no references to Central High.

In July a surprise came through my office door in the arms of my darling daughter Celia. Before presenting her treasure, Celia described the fun times she had with her brother Trammell looking through family papers, curious about their ancestors. The book she carried was a leather-bound volume with the embossed gilt title *The Girl's Memory Book*. It was a worn, well-loved volume stuffed with ephemera and photographs. Celia brought us firsthand records to complement our efforts to retrace Aunt Mary's life. This book encapsulated Mary's life in 1922 at Central High School. Her memory book and yearbook the *Aegis*, gave us a thorough account of her last year in high school.

The memory book began with a picture of my father, Wash Bryan "Tex" Trammell. Evidence of the bond between Aunt Mary and Dad has survived long beyond their lifetimes. After Aunt Mary passed away in 1968, Tex dutifully kept her belongings until his death in 1988. No matter the time, it seems that Mary kept track of her brother and all his activities, and he features all throughout her scrapbooks. My father was always a dynamic person—at any event, he was at the center of the crowd, riveting others with animated conversation. He also kept mementos from his school days and friend inscriptions attested to his effect on people. During his time at Culver Military Academy, Tex was singled out for his excellence in football. The following was noted in the 1921 campus yearbook, the *Culver Roll Call*: "*Although he was laid out of the game with a broken arm for five weeks, he had the guts to play in the Lake Forest game when his arm had just been taken out of the sling. He was one of the best halfbacks we had. Whenever a gain was needed Trammell was given the ball.*"

Photograph

Center of attraction as per usua

Aunt Mary's notations contain lively words. She was a wordsmith and developed into a fine journalist. Her attitude towards life was energetic and humorous. Her brother was a boisterous youth, as handsome as he was physically talented.

Tex and a couple of his Culver Military Academy comrades. I saw this laughing face of my father's many times.

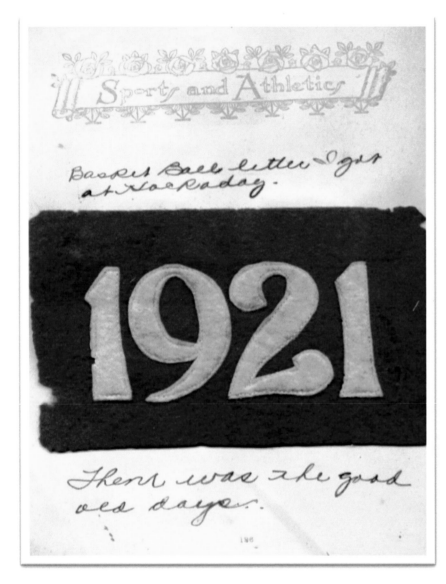

Pasted in the Central High memory book was her Hockaday letter for basketball. Aunt Mary was a head taller than many of her competitors which helped her achieve success on the basketball court.

Athletically inclined like her brother, Aunt Mary play on the Hockaday basketball team at Kent Place School. In September of 1922, at Central High School she was elected captain of the basketball team. Although she was a newcomer to Central, the memory book show that her personality and exuberance won her the respect of many.

Mary played the center position and in a 1922 newspaper the following was recorded- "'Central Quintets Take Two Games.' The boys' and girls' basketball teams of Central High scored a double victory over Ball High of Galveston on the Central Y.M.C.A. court in Houston Wednesday. The local boys defeated their island rivals 32 to 22 and the girls followed up this victory by winning 27 to 12. At Central Thursday there was an informal reception that tendered the winning athletes before classes started."

Aunt Mary's memory book has 200 pages of fond sentiments and original prose. She pasted in season ticket stubs to Central High School basketball games along with newspaper accounts of basketball victories. There are black and yellow ribbons, a Thanksgiving Hop dance card, florist gift cards, congratulatory telegrams sent via the Rice Hotel, banquet guest cards, and a 1922 season ticket receipt which allowed her access to "all base-ball games and track events held exclusively under the auspices of the Athletic Council of the Central High School- Price One Dollar."

Capt Trammell

The 1922 *Aegis* published that *"Mary Trammell, together with her team, had a very successful season. She displayed lots of fight during the season".*

OUR SPONSOR

Miss Gussie Howard

Words can express but a small part of our esteem for our Aegis Sponsor.

Many faculty members took the time to write in Mary's book. They mention enjoying Mary's wit, humor, leadership, and the faith that she would accomplish great things in life.

Gussie Howard wrote in Mary's book,

"A friend may well be reckoned the master piece of nature."

Very Sincerely,

Gussie Howard

"Dear Mary,

I do not know what I shall do without you. You know I have gotten so accustomed to your dropping in every few days to tell me about your troubles.

Seriously though, we shall miss you and you leave Central with our very best wishes for a happy and useful future. You are capable of doing big things in the world and we will be disappointed if you do not.

Do not forget Old Central and your sincere friend."

F. M. Black

Prof. F. M. Black

Everyone knows the character of this wonderful man.

Principal F. M. Black noticed Mary's ability as a leader.

The student section of her memory book is filled with friendly notes beside pasted cameo photographs of the author. A common theme among their sentiments was Aunt Mary's humor, spunk and character.

On a card pasted onto one page is the anonymous message,

"Here's to Mary Trammell

So faithful and True

Long may you live

With this cupid for you."

The value of Celia's memory book discovery is illustrated by the anonymous saying *"show me your friends and I'll you who you are."* The memory book is three-quarters filled with revealing comments about Aunt Mary. The sentiments are from students and faculty members. We spent hours deciphering faint, handwritten notes in the *Girl Graduate's Memory Book* and matching the authors with portraits from the *Aegis* yearbook. Of all the messages, John Robertson's seemed to be the perfect sample to begin.

April 26, 1922

Dear Mary,
This is a time when we think of Central more than during the past three years. I feel like I am writing in a book belonging to Central itself, because in all school activities you were taking the lead and putting it thru. It is said that you carry great weight at Central We all think a whole lot of Central and though we of course are glad that the time for graduation has come, we hate to leave it. When afterward I think of the school I will be thinking of a Mary Trammell, a jolly, good natured girl, with a grin that reaches from ear to ear.

John Robertson

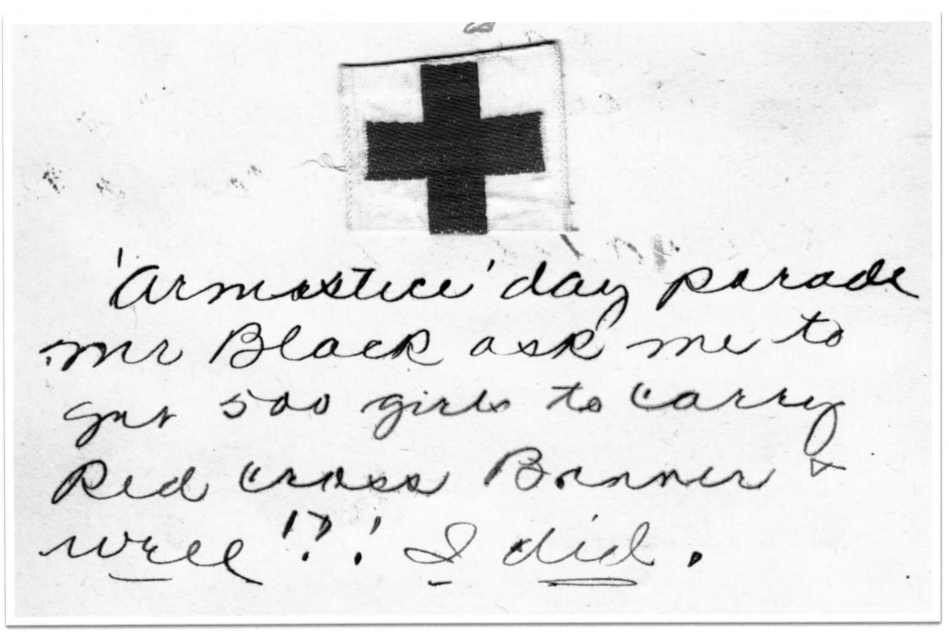

'Armistice' day parade
Mr Black ask me to
get 500 girls to carry
Red cross Banner &
well!?! I did.

Mr. F. M. Black's challenge was successfully accepted by Aunt Mary. She was able to inspire many others to participate.

Mary Darling,
It's so hard to write what I really want to say
Mary. I don't know how to tell you how I've
loved knowing and being with you this last year
of school—
But our friendship would end here Mary, but it
can't it we both go to Rice. With all the love and
bestest wishes a good old friend can wish to you
Bushels and oceans of love--------
Frances Sellers

Dearest Mary,
Although in reality I've known you only a short while
it seems as if it's been nearly always, doesn't it?
We're both tennis sharks more or less aren't we?
And, too, we were both were on the right side for cap
and gowns. Now there are two perfectly good
reasons why we'll keep on being as good friends as
always as we are now—eh what?
Well, I'm wishing you just loads of good luck all thru
your life and I know you'll have it too. 'Cause look
who you are and how you started out.   You're all
right Mary J. Trammell!

You're friend, Mary Margaret Forbes

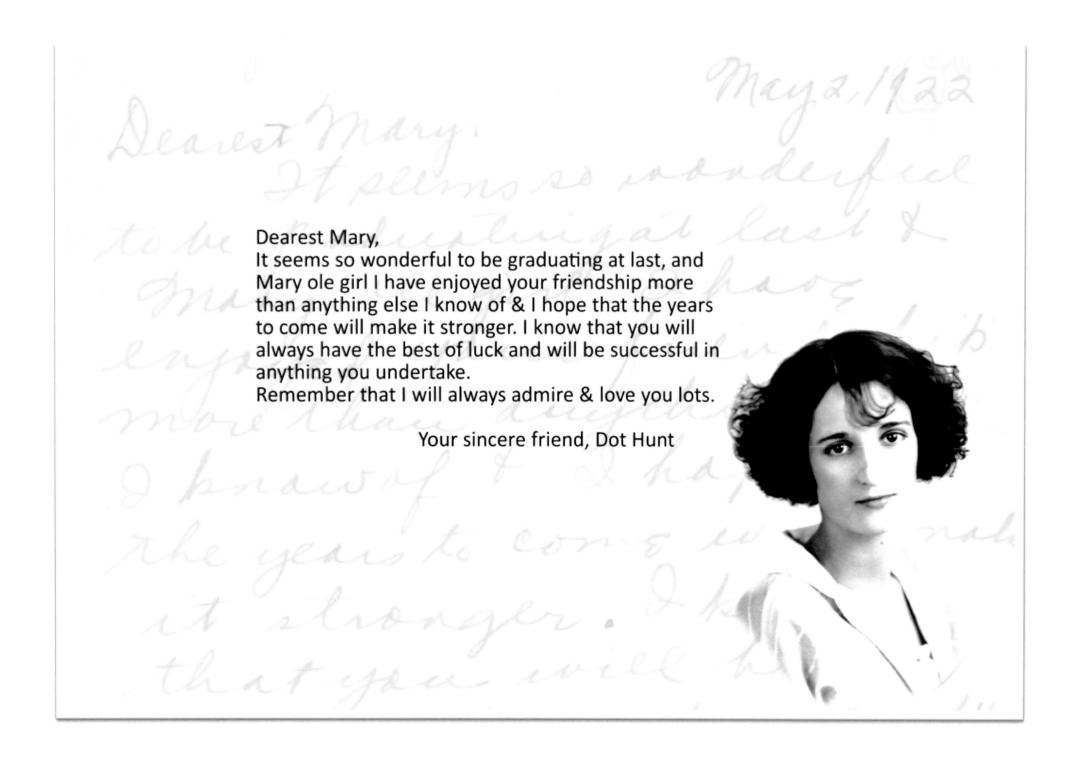

Dearest Mary,
It seems so wonderful to be graduating at last, and Mary ole girl I have enjoyed your friendship more than anything else I know of & I hope that the years to come will make it stronger. I know that you will always have the best of luck and will be successful in anything you undertake.
Remember that I will always admire & love you lots.

Your sincere friend, Dot Hunt

My Dearest Mary

It is extremely difficult for me to write what I would like in the book of one I have loved so much. You really don't know how much I've enjoyed friendship even though it has only been for a very short time. Much shorter than I wish so I sincerely hope it will not end with graduation. My I wish you all the happiness that this will hold and I hope everything will come your way in life

Always remember Ol' Ilfrey.
Love and best wishes
Marjorie Ilfrey

Dearest

if you don't know how crazy I am about you, you're not as dumb as you look, you're dumber. I can't tell you what your friendship has meant and always will mean to me. I know that this is pretty punk especially after waiting two weeks to write it. But please accept it as the best of a poor fool.

Forever yours,

Frank

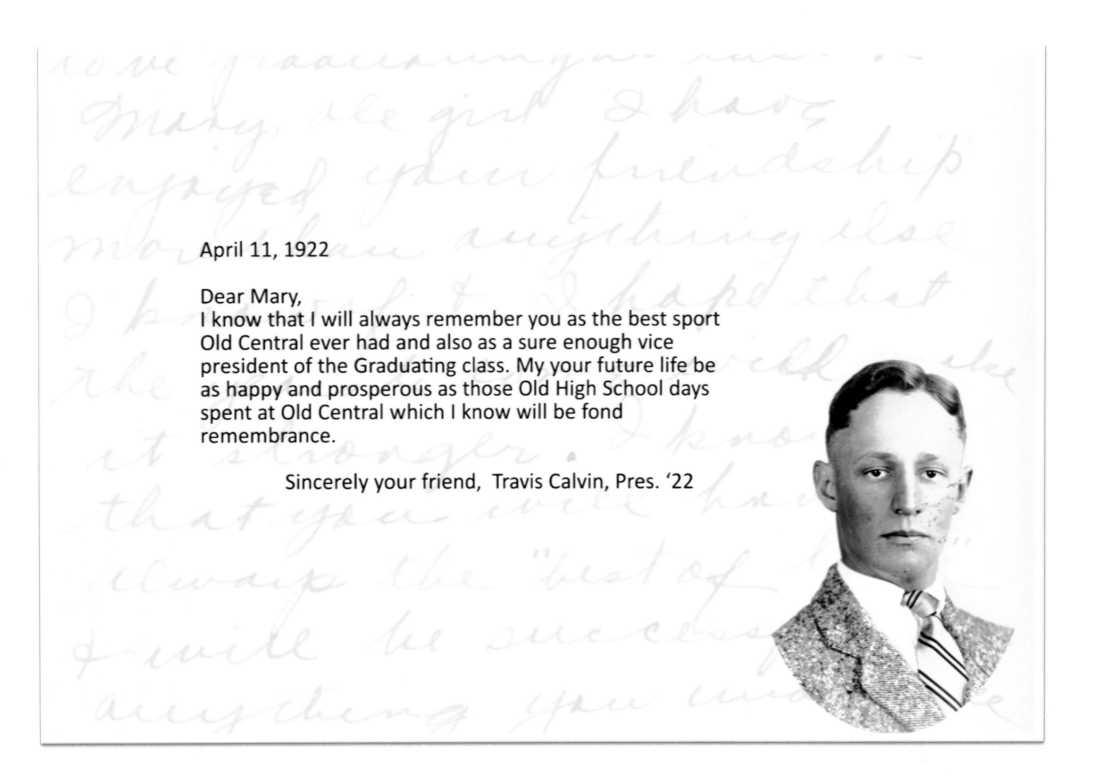

April 11, 1922

Dear Mary,
I know that I will always remember you as the best sport
Old Central ever had and also as a sure enough vice
president of the Graduating class. My your future life be
as happy and prosperous as those Old High School days
spent at Old Central which I know will be fond
remembrance.

    Sincerely your friend, Travis Calvin, Pres. '22

Justine sitting on Mary's "Little Hupp" front hood

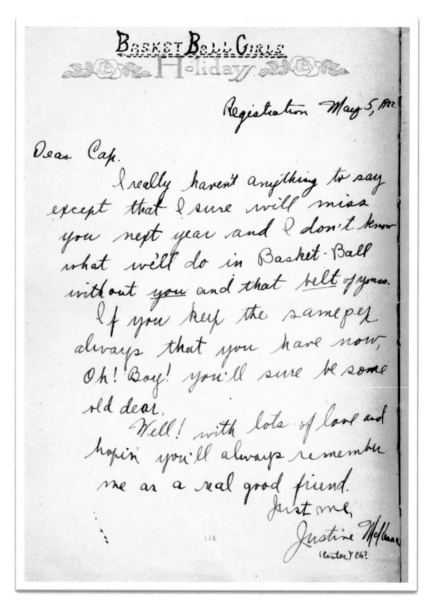

Aunt Mary always had a quick and endearing mile. She had the loyalty of all she met. Whether in Houston, College Station, San Antonio, Galveston, or Clear Lake, she and her friends were always on the go. Aunt Mary drove one of the first cars at Central High School and it was always piled high with revelers.

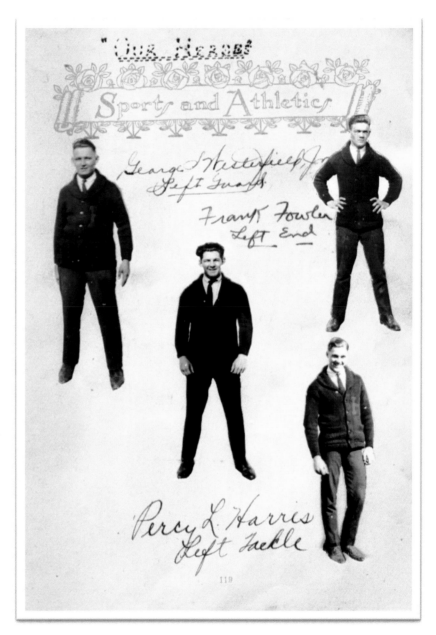

Aunt Mary's artistic and painstaking design on these pages is repeated throughout the Central High memory book.

Aunt Mary was a great supporter of "Old Centrals" sports teams and her enthusiasm did not go unnoticed.

Dear Captain Mary,

Well old girl so you are leaving us. Well I am certainly sorry for several reasons. While trotting up and down the hall it will seem very dark without your everlasting bright beaming smile. Then too, Old Central will miss you too on their basketball team and you rooting at all their games. I want to wish you all the happiness and health and success in the world and always remember. Orin G. Henley

Darling Mary, April 12, 1922

That's what they all say. How do you expect me to write while you are fighting? But after all is said and done I will still remember Mary as a sport among sports and may you think of me when you feel lonesome and don't forget my phone number S.O.S.?

Richard Wray

BEAUTY AND POPULARITY CONTEST

THERE is nothing new under the sun, but the *Aegis'* "Popularity and Beauty Contest" was an innovation in Central High School. Central students were given opportunity to select the prettiest girl in the school. Miss Mildred Ennen was accorded this honor. Miss Mary Trammell was selected Central's most popular girl by a large majority.

Percy Harris was chosen Central's handsomest boy over a field of seven candidates. Vic Andrew was selected most popular boy.

Considerable interest was manifested in the contest, which lasted two weeks.

. Vic Andrew, the most popular boy, wrote the following inscription in her memory book.

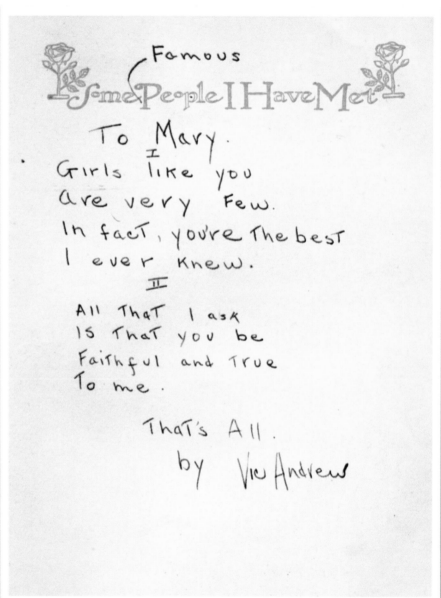

Famous
Some People I Have Met

To Mary.

I

Girls like you
are very few.
In fact, you're the best
I ever knew.

II

All that I ask
is that you be
faithful and true
to me.

That's All.

by Vic Andrew

Every year the student body picked the winners. Even though Aunt Mary entered Central High as a senior, her personality successfully propelled her from a virtually unknown student to most popular girl

Mildred Ennen - Prettiest Girl

Mary Trammell - Most Popular Girl

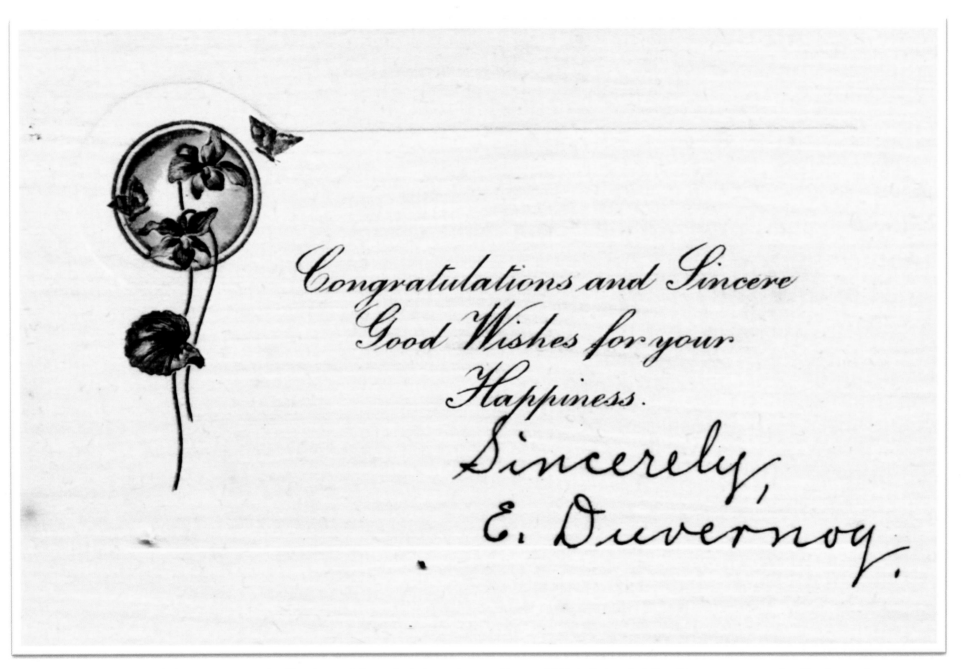

Congratulations and Sincere Good Wishes for your Happiness.

Sincerely,

E. Duvernoy.

Aunt Mary gained the respect and affection of the administration at Central High School. Miss Duvernoy was the Registrar in 1922.

Rice Institute was almost a decade old when Aunt Mary Jane appeared on campus. She had spent the summer traveling between Houston, Dallas, Abilene, and Hamlin. Many of her friends from Central High also attended Rice, though for Mary no one was a stranger for long.

My grandparents were not surprised that Mary embraced college and all its facets. She started right from the beginning with a very public profile, running for student government and making many new friends. Mary loved athletics and supported the Owl's sports teams both on the field and in the stands. She herself played a sharp game of tennis. As a freshman, she played her way to the 1923 championship finals. After she joined the Elizabeth Baldwin Literary Society (EBLS),where one of the members pledges turned out to be Susie Ella Fondren, Mary's future sister-in-law and my mother. Susie's sister Katherine also joined the EBLS a few years later.

Rice University's campus newspaper has been student-run since its first publication in 1916 as *The Thresher*. Ever the extravert, Aunt's Mary's name appeared in *The Thresher* more than a few times. These papers can still be found today as digitized scans in the Fondren Library's Woodson Research Center.

Feb 1923 "Thoughts and Sights While Strolling Around Rice.' Even the girls are throwing at the line—Corinne, a petite little lass, leads them in the fray. Our friend Trammell received a broken finger when she went to pick up some shekels that belonged to Corinne."

From the recollections of those who knew her and experienced her humor, Mary was always charismatic and pleasant company. She avidly supported her school's sports teams, once driving her car to College Station packed full of students to cheer on an Owl football game. Fay and Barney Morton supported her soial ventures in grand style. The Rice Hotel was a very popular venue among Rice students.

Bessie Smith

One particular friend of Mary's was Bessie Smith, who was known across campus for her journalism and photography. Her pictures appear throughout the scrapbook. A photographer for the student paper, *The Thresher* staff published a fond farewell when she took an editorial position for the school yearbook.

The 1922 *Thresher* reported,

"Bessie Smith was appointed Associate Editor of the Campanile. *Miss Smith will be remembered for her excellent work as Staff Photographer of* The Thresher *and Snapshot."*

"After the jubilee the gang got back somehow and I'll tell the world that the distance between the Rice Hotel and Rice Institute is not less than ten miles at 4 a.m. The Crusaders numbered about forty with the dorms contributing about half, the Autry's and Nelms' cars about twelve, and Mary Trammell the remainder of the party."

Another headline read *"Wine, Women and Song and 'Men' Appear at Dance"* and the event description states *"M. J. Trammell had two dates!!"*

Mary and Bessie had many friends in common and participated in equally entertaining activities.

From the *Thresher* in 1922

" TATTLERS TAKE UP AQUATICS

The feature of the day was a daring plunge into the pool by Miss Mildred Miller, who showed herself quite impassive to the risk of

immersing herself entirely in the water. Other members of the club looked on astonished at the feat. Miss Bessie Smith wore a ruffled

taffeta divers' costume with African beauty trimming. Miss Mildred Miller was in sky blue oat sacking with garlands of fresh radishes."

"Rice Institute of the 1920s continued to be a small undergraduate college with high academic standards for mainly Texas-born students. Student life on

campus drew more focus in the early '20s with an increase in visiting lecturers, the Rice Engineering Show showcasing exhibits, and the festive May Fete. Student

hazing continued to be a part of the male-dominated population and freshmen, including women, were called "Slimes." Rice men, spurred on by brooms and belts,

paraded down Main Street annually between 1923 and 1927 to the Rice Hotel until the event was abolished in 1928. Students were concerned with meals and

clothing; food was so bad that a foot riot ensued with the administration levying a fine of $37 on each diner. Fashion called for canes, derbies and wing collars. Two

residential halls were available for men, but women had no living quarters on Rice and only a room in the Administration Building for studying and relaxing. Lunch

could be eaten with men in the commons or on the grounds, but women had to be off campus by 5:00 p.m. All courses were open to both men and women and all

students signed the honor system pledge for examinations." -Lee Pecht, Rice University Archivist & Director of Special Collections

Another good friend of Mary's was John Hornbuckle, editor of the student yearbook the *Campanile*. Just like Mary, he had a strong school spirit and disliked the apathy of the student body. This led him to write a feisty letter to the editor of *The Thresher*.

"The staff is endeavoring to make the 1923 Campanile commemorative of the Tenth Anniversary of Rice and while they do not make any extravagant claims for it, they state that there will be several new features this year and a fuller treatment of some phases of Rice that should make for a more interesting book... There seems to be an attitude that by having one's picture taken for the Campanile *he renders the* Campanile *and its staff a great favor. This is not the case. If makes no difference to the staff whether students get their pictures made or not...." He replaced the former editor mid-year and was trying to complete the yearbook by graduation. The Campanile is the record of each student's life at Rice, and without a picture in the Class section this cannot be complete, for in a great many cases that is the only trace of his or her attendance."*

Aunt Mary, Mac, and an unidentified friend in Galveston.

Aunt Mary was a member of the Rice Dramatic Club and performed in *The Double Demon*, directed by Chauncey Stewart. The play is set in a courtroom where a jury of eleven women and one man deliberate on the case of a man arrested for kissing a young lady, a stranger to him, on a park bench. The jury deadlocks twice: first, when a juror votes "not guilty," and later when an attractive female juror convinces him to change his mind, only to find his wife, the forewoman, disagreeing. Mary played the forewoman.

Hugh St John Murray

She had a hand in many campus projects, whether it was leading the charge to sell more ads for the *Campanile* yearbook, or organizing a swanky party at the Rice Hotel to raise money for the Rice Owl band's new uniforms where they raised $1,000—about $13,800 in today's money.

Aunt Mary was an advocate for women's rights, and a women's liberation proponent long before the term was coined. While at Rice Institute, she was managing editor of the *Co-Ed Thresher* for its debut issue. The female students felt the need to be represented in their own way. One of the most impressive accomplishments was her election as the first female councilman-at-large of the Rice Student Council.

She was given an endorsement by *The Thresher*—*"Mary Trammell We feel that the co-eds of Rice are deserving of representation on the Student Council other than through vice-president. We feel that this additional representative should be someone especially fitted to the position. In view of the large part she has taken in co-ed activities and the well-deserved leadership which she has gained, we recommend the election Monday of Mary J. Trammell as councilman-at-large."*

Signed H.F. Ander, W.J. Grace, H.S. Murray, and Taft Lyons

J. Lonnie Thomas

Aunt Mary had many friends but did not leave winning for councilman-at-large up to chance. The morning of the election several hundred posters were distributed among the thousand students. She won by the highest number of votes cast in the election for any office—315. Her opponent received 129.

Mary celebrated life in all its dimensions. She never just sat back and observed, she acted and led. This section introduces the characters who also roamed the Rice Institute campus from 1922 to 1926 and to whom Aunt Mary brought her customary joy and laughter. This handsome man is J. Lonnie Thomas from Greenville, Texas. He appears several times in Mary's scrapbook. Rice Institute's yearbook, the 1924 *Campanile*, published a special note beside his track picture.

"Consistent practice and hard work won a letter for Thomas, whose specialty was the javelin throw. Thomas was not a star, but was a reliable field man, taking second place often in his event."

I heard once that Aunt Mary fell in love with a young man and brought him to Sweetwater to meet her father, Walter. He liked her choice quite well. Her mother Fay disapproved. The identity of this beau is a family mystery, but Lonnie would have made a handsome choice. Aunt Mary never married.

Captain Alphus ("Maggie") McGee

Thresher News – "Alphus ("Maggie") McGee of Abilene was awarded his varsity letter by Coach Phil Arbuckle, who said that the team of 1922 *"has given to the limit more than any Rice team has....Several Rice backs have been tackled within the five-yard line but, thanks to the mud, have slid across the goal for a touchdown. Graves (Maggie) McGee was famous for that."*

Mac was one of Mary's good friends who appears in many photographs and articles in *The Thresher*. He was often a passenger in her "Little Hupp" automobile driving between football games, College Station, Galveston, and the Rice Hotel. According to Rice University archivist Lee Pecht, in 1922 there were around 154 cars on Rice Institute's campus.

Aunt Mary and friends enjoyed the drive to Clear Lake to spend a lazy afternoon near the water.

The smile on Aunt Mary's face remained bright and welcoming her entire life. She had an exuberant personality that attracted people.

Noel Charles Willis

Aunt Mary enjoyed all sports, but basketball was definitely her favorite.

The Campanile

"Noel Charles Willis from Denton, TX President's Student Association 23-24, Senior Cane Cmte., Basketball 22-24-Captain 23-24; Sports Editor Senior Thresher. An all-around basketball players was Captain Willis, perfectly as ease at forward, center, or guard, and very efficient in each position. To say that he was popular with his teammates can be illustrated by the fact that he served the Owl Cagers for two years as their captain. This feat has only been done about twice in the history of Rice athletics. Noel was a basketball player of great stamina, he was ever on the job and led the pace for his teammates. Captain Willis' services will be greatly missed next year when graduation will sever his connections with Rice in June."

According to Lee Pecht, Rice University Archivist and Director, during the time when Aunt Mary attended Rice Institute, "Athletics were an integral part of campus life as Rice was a charter member of the Southwest Conference for football, basketball, track, and baseball. Everyone walked, cycled, or took the trolley to and from campus, from the President and professors to the students, but there were cars and it was reported that an average of 154 cars daily appeared on campus."

CAMPBELL, "*Bubba*"
Houston, Texas

"Bubba," too, played his last game for the Gray and Blue on Thanksgiving day, even if it was for only one play. He received a twisted ankle in the Southwestern game which rendered him valueless for the rest of the season. This made "Bubba's" third year at end, he played a hard, consistent game, driving all the time. A fast man and a good tackler, it was rare, indeed, when the opposing team made a gain around his wing.

WILLIS, "*Norah*"
Denton, Texas

Another senior lineman, weighing only 170, but tough as a bull and as hard to move as a brick wall. "Cap" played the position of left tackle, and played with his head up. He had a natural love for man-sized football and practiced on each opposing tackle, much to the latter's discomfort. He showed the same fight on the gridiron as he did on the basketball court, and made as enviable a reputation for himself as a footballer as he did as captain of the basketball team for two years.

Campanile page for Noel Willis

J. Lonnie and Noel Willis in the Rice
Campus Parking Area

The *Thresher* in March of 1923 published this memo- *"We want to advise "Fat" Heflin and young Dangliesan to look before they leap at boulevard auto rides, offered especially by good looking women. Keep those eyes open for snares, my chaps.*

The *Campanile* lists William Cecil "Fats" Heflin from Temple, TX Football 22-24, "R" Association, Student athletic rep 25-26, "Queen" of the Men's May fete, 1924.

Aunt Mary's picture of two good friends J. Lonnie and Fats

Fats the Timekeeper

The January 1924 *Thresher* announced. *"Palmer 'Peg' Melton is to coach the freshman baseball team this season, He says that not much material is on hand."*

Peg was an excellent ball player and captain of the team. Aunt Mary with her extensive knowledge of baseball history admired him greatly. He appears several times in her scrapbooks.

Aunt Mary's photograph of Peg Melton

The *Thresher* reported *"Frank Goss is an old Rice Star in the 220-yard dash, winning many points for the Owls in that event. He had been in the 440 many times taking first or second place."*

Aunt Mary's photograph at the finish line of Frank Goss

Mary's caption for this picture was *"That Squad That Beat A & M"*

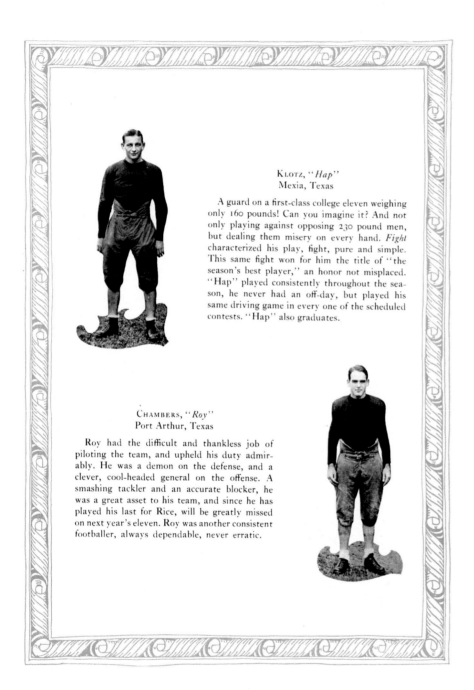

KLOTZ, "Hap"
Mexia, Texas

A guard on a first-class college eleven weighing only 160 pounds! Can you imagine it? And not only playing against opposing 230 pound men, but dealing them misery on every hand. *Fight* characterized his play, fight, pure and simple. This same fight won for him the title of "the season's best player," an honor not misplaced. "Hap" played consistently throughout the season, he never had an off-day, but played his same driving game in every one of the scheduled contests. "Hap" also graduates.

CHAMBERS, "Roy"
Port Arthur, Texas

Roy had the difficult and thankless job of piloting the team, and upheld his duty admirably. He was a demon on the defense, and a clever, cool-headed general on the offense. A smashing tackler and an accurate blocker, he was a great asset to his team, and since he has played his last for Rice, will be greatly missed on next year's eleven. Roy was another consistent footballer, always dependable, never erratic.

Aunt Mary loved sports and so did her family. Her scrapbooks are filled with action shots of friends on the Rice Institute fields.

Dutchy and Roy

Susie Ella Fondren and her brother Walter William Fondren in 1924 at Rice Institute

Campanile Vanity Fair section highlighted Susie Fondren

One of Mary's close friends at Rice Institute was the beauty Susie Ella Fondren. She and her brother Walter Fondren were in the grade just below Mary, but through membership in the Elizabeth Baldwin Literary Society the girls became good friends. Countless announcements of events hosted by Fay and Mary at the Rice Hotel were published in the *Galveston Daily News* and *Houston Post*. These articles described elaborate table settings and guest gifts. One particular luncheon was given in honor of Susie Fondren, my mother.

The *Galveston Daily News* reported that *"Miss Mary Trammell is entertaining with a 1 o'clock luncheon at the Rice Hotel Thursday, honoring Miss Susie Fondren."* The reception was to celebrate Susie's election as *"Queen of the May Fete"*. In 1924, Susie appeared in the Vanity Fair section of the Campanile. She was a blue-eyed beauty with the perfect look for the popular bob-cut hairstyle and type of dress. As Queen of the May Fete she had duties to perform. Susie was chairman of the banquet committee and the final ball was set for Monday June 6 at the Rice Hotel

The *Galveston Daily News* reported,

"Miss Susie Fondren entertained Saturday at River Oaks Country Club with a large luncheon for members of the Elizabeth Baldwin Literary Society. The guests were seated at a long table decorated in club colors of lavender and white. Covers for 36 were marked by unique favors in the way of linen handkerchiefs on which the names were hand embroidered. Miss Fondren was assisted in hostess duties by her mother Mrs. W. W. Fondren."

It is through Mary Trammell and Susie Fondren's friendship that my story continues. My mother Susie lived at 3410 Montrose with her parents Ella and Walter William, a brother Walter William, Jr., and a younger sister Mary Catherine. The twenty-one room home was built by my grandparents so that extended family would always have a place to gather and at times live together.

Rice Institute students had active social schedules. Aunt Mary and my mother did many activities together, and it was through this association that my parents first met. The City of Houston by 1920 had expanded to an area of thirty-eight miles. There were air-conditioned movies theaters like The Majestic. It was just a short ride to the warm waters of Galveston Bay or the reactional spot of Sylvan Beach, noted for its picnics and live music at the Pavilion. It was at some party that Tex and Susie became better acquainted.

Mary Catherine, Walter William, and Susie Ella Fondren during their early college years.

Aunt Mary used to tell us, "*Sweetie lived at 3410 Montrose and Tex and I would pick her up and venture around Houston. After one night, Tex drove to the Rice Hotel and opened the door and said "Goodbye Mary." I got out, they drove off, and that was the last time they ever took me on a date with them.*"

"Sweetie" was my mother's nickname because she was the nicest person to all she met. Tex and Sweetie, my parents married the year after she graduated from college. Family was always important to Aunt Mary and she instilled the same feelings in me and my brothers through her attention and avid storytelling.

Me (Mary Trammell) and "Pud" Young

Aunt Mary had the resources and enthusiasm for travel. Ever the young journalist, she loved to record her adventures with candid and staged photography. One scrapbook we uncovered had postcard-worthy photographs of Yellowstone National Park in Wyoming, and the Stapp's Lake Ranch in Colorado. These places of natural beauty were a perfect backdrop for her practicing her photography and chronicling her youth. Written below many of the photographs are playful captions, perhaps written while in Abilene or at the Y6 ranch kitchen table. Page by page, Mary chronicled her travels with friends through Wyoming and Colorado, stopping to add captions like "A dog named Thor," "The Corn Cabin," and "The Twain of Us."

The pages to follow have her candid and original photographs of Yellowstone National Park and the Minerva Spring and Terrace at Mammoth. This site is popular for striking bright colors and ornate travertine formations. Early stewards of Yellowstone believed that automobiles were loud, smoky, and scared the horses, so tourists had to use horses or buggies to view the attractions. Progress and expansion overruled these regulations, and by 1923 large touring buses carrying eleven passengers each were seen around the park. By 1925, some vehicles could transport up to twenty-five people. Eventually private cars were also available to rent. It was in the early 1920s that the National Park Service began giving out ten-year contracts to companies supplying services and goods. At the time of Mary's visit it was a popular destination for travelers around the world

Minerva Spring has a recorded temperature of 161°F.

"Buffalo Bill 'Cody' Dam is a concrete arch-gravity dam on the Shoshone River in the U.S. state of Wyoming. It is named after the famous Wild West figure William 'Buffalo Bill' Cody, who founded the nearby town of Cody. Buffalo Bill also owned much of the land now covered by the reservoir formed by ts construction." U.S. Bureau of Reclamation

Left to Right- Two perspectives of Cody Canyon and Cody Dam.

Old Faithful Inn

"Old Faithful at its best."

The Yellowstone Park Company's architect Robert Reamer designed this structure in 1902 and the construction was completed by 1904. By the time of Mary's visit, the inn had been expanded and modified several times. In 1913 the east wing was added to the 120-room original structure, and in 1922 the dining room was enlarged.

An early version of a tour bus, to take people through the park.

Aunt Mary is seated

Our first tent canyon

Gladys Ross　　　　　On Yellowstone Dam

"One of the fascinating things about the Old Faithful Inn is the visitors' reactions to the structure. Upon being informed of its age, most assume that this massive log and stone lodge was standard fare in a national park circa 1900. They couldn't be more mistaken...The average park lodging at the turn of the 20th Century consisted of ramshackle, hastily built rectangular structures with undersized rooms and unimaginative designs. Construction was typically shoddy, and fire safety was dreadfully lacking. Most park visitors arrived after hours in a jarring carriage ride. They were hungry and exhausted; the typical road hotels provided large meals, a warm fire, and a very small room—all sufficient. Larger, more luxurious hotels often presented a Colonial or some revival facade, and overly machined Victorian decor within. While these hotels were a bit rough by today's standards, they hardly looked like rugged lodges."

National Park Lodge Architecture Society

CodyRuth and me in 1886

Little Judy Jones Matthews with her cousin Mary Jane.

Thankfully, Aunt Mary enjoyed recording her journeys. She would have made a wonderful photojournalist and we are better off for her persistence.

These pictures were taken while horseback riding, swimming, and enjoying the city of Ward Colorado in 1922.

The Train of us   Mary Duggan   *Alone*   Little Lake

Viola Coombs Stapp, Marion Briggs Me- Leon Luther - Our 1st trip up.

Aunt Mary and "Mammam" were both fond of livestock and horses. She poses for this picture in Colorado while on vacation with some Rice Institute

Thomas Trammell

Married in 1872, Thomas Trammell and his beautiful bride Mary Jane Newman were both from West Texas ranching families. Mary Jane was his first wife and the mother of his three sons. She was known for her exquisite taste and beautiful wardrobe. Their large home in Sweetwater was occasionally used as a sanitary place for surgical procedures.

Thomas Trammell's impact on horse breeding in Texas and the United States has had a long term effect. There are horses today that have Trammell blood and are superior animals. Trammell moved to Sweetwater and two years later opened the first bank and called it the Trammell Bank. He was also responsible for bringing the railroad lines through Sweetwater.

Mary Jane Newman Trammell

In 1880, my maternal great-grandparents Sam Cook Young and Julia 'Jennie' Bryan were married. On the left is a picture of them before marriage. Sam Cook Young was a rancher and Jennie was the daughter of Colonel Washington Carroll Bryan, also a rancher. She eventually inherited one-third of the 20,000 acre T-Diamond Ranch. The house they lived in at 601 Amarillo in Abilene is now owned by a local Abilene historian.

"To love Abilene history and to just so happen to live in the very home that Sue's great-grandparents built is a wonderful bit of parallelism! We are proud to call Sam and Julia Young's home, our home and equally proud to have that connection with Sue Trammell and her family."

Jay Taylor Moore

Sam Cook Young and Julia 'Jennie' Bryan

Julia 'Jennie' Young and Sam Young

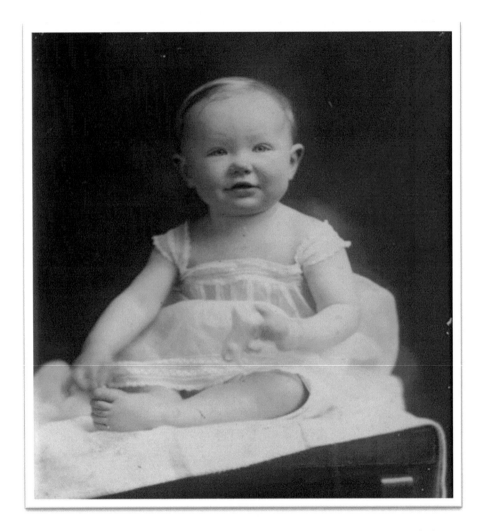

Here is my grandmother, Fay Young Morton. The ability to garner others respect continued throughout her life where at the Y6 ranch, the cowboys lovingly called her 'Madame Queen'.

Fay Young Morton about 1920 while living at the
Rice Hotel

After her marriage to Barney B. Morton, she dropped the Trammell name, and was known as Fay Young Morton. She was an accomplished bridge player and hosted, entered and won tournaments. During her residency at the Rice Hotel many events, including bridge games were held in the Crystal Ballroom. At the Y6 ranch, she placed all of her bridge trophies along a ledge below the ceiling. Most visitors assumed they were won by her famous Hereford cattle and complimented her on her success as a breeder. "Mammam", forever a gracious hostess, did not contradict her guests and they were none the wiser.

Fay Young Trammell c.1906

Walter during his marriage to Fay.

Walter Thomas Trammell at 17 years old. He was living in Sweetwater, working at the Trammell Bank.

College Days

Susie Ella "Sweetie" Fondren-My Mother

Mary Jane Trammell- My Aunt Mary

Wash Bryan "Tex" Trammell – My Father

Aunt Mary and my father Tex were competitive athletes. She always had pictures of him in her scrapbooks with funny inscriptions like "Bud", or "Of course". They adored each other.

The Corsicana Daily Sun on September 8, 1924 reported- *"Invitations have been issued to approximately 100 University of Texas students to attend the fall training camp... on the same day, Mrs. D. B. Emmons, of Austin, will begin serving meals at the training table for the athletes. All members of the squad will be required to eat at her table during the training camp and during the football season. The following students are listed: .....W.B. Trammell, Houston."*

Me, Aunt Mary, Mother

Dad,"Momo", "Sweety"

Aunt Mary and Mother remained good friends as well as sisters-in-law. My family has always been close-knit and I attribute this to my two grandmother's and their focus on family unity. I love this picture of mother with a smile on her face. She was very formal in pictures and rarely smiled. In life, she lived up to her nickname "Sweetie" and was adored by her children. She was very close to her widowed mother, Ella Cochrum Fondren "Momo" and they talked by phone at least twice a day my entire life. My grandfather Walter William Fondren died in 1939 and 'Momo' lived until 1982.

Four Generations of the Family

In 1957 this picture was taken with the newest Trammell addition. Great-grandmother Fay Morton (standing right) and grandfather Tex Trammell (left) gathered at the Whitfield home to welcome baby Susan Trammell Whitfield. This was a joyous occasion which brought together multiple generations of my family.

Aunt Mary was a constant in our lives up to her death in 1968. All family events were made special by her inclusion. My parents, Tex and Sweetie, loved her and this was passed onto to me and my brothers, Tom and Bryan. In this photograph, Bryan and Aunt Mary pose at one of their fabulous theme parties. Even as teenagers, we loved being around her humor, wit, and relaxed outlook on life.

Chapter 6
West Texas Memories

West Texas cactus and barbed wire.

To some people West Texas is synonymous with cactus, barbed wire, cattle and dust. To the Trammell family, West Texas means pride, a long standing relationship with the arid land, and appreciation for the persistence of our ancestors. Primary source materials like the pictures in this book are priceless and I am privileged to be "keeper of the records" for this generation of the Trammell clan. An entire room in my home has been designated to house the "Family Collection". Scrapbooks, letters, pictures and other ephemera line the shelves and cabinets. A lifetime of gathered family information is in the process of being archived and labeled. My office has fifteen shelves of photos and cabinets of individual genealogical files beginning with me as File One and my parents are Two and Three. This continues for approximately three centuries of ancestors back to the *Mayflower*.

The Trammell's were and are a close knit clan. Our early female ancestors, along with their men, settled the plains of Texas. Sophia was born in St. Augustine, Texas when it was still a territory and her daughter Julia and her siblings lived near or with each other for most of their lives. Julia and her daughter Fay, both widowed a year apart, lived together in Abilene and at the Y6 ranch. When Aunt Mary returned to Abilene, she lived near Fay, and years later they moved in together. I am happy to report that two of my four children are here in Texas, and my West Coast sons visit quite often. Family is of the utmost importance to me but I do sometimes wish we all lived as I did on Bluebonnet Street with cousins no further than a backyard away. I have three grandsons and three granddaughters. My precious family members mean more to me than I can adequately express.

Sophia Wyres Bryan (1837-1904)

Julia "Jennie" Bryan (1862-1947)

Fay Young Morton (1881-1869)

Aunt Mary's life began in Sweetwater, so Susan and I decided to get reacquainted with this West Texas town. We flew to Abilene one early June morning and checked into the Sayles Ranch Guesthouse at 942 Amarillo Street. This was a fitting accommodation from which to launch our travels. "Cottage Clare" just happened to be three blocks away from where my great-grandparents Sam and Jennie Young lived. Their house at 601 Amarillo is now owned by Laura and Jay Moore. They invited us into their home and we were delighted to walk the spaces that once held many gracious and memorable parties hosted by the Young family. Laura is the Executive Director of the Grace Museum while Jay teaches history at Abilene High School. He is the creator of History in Plain Sight, a film series documenting Abilene's past. Abilene was host to a large contingent of our family. On Sam Young's 80th birthday, three hundred guests were invited to his daughter Laura Legett's country home on Hereford Lake, located seven miles east of Abilene on the Bankhead highway. Members of the Young, Legett, Jones and Bryan families were in attendance and an announcement of the festivities was published by the *Abilene Reporter News*.

601 Amarillo built in 1924

This photo was taken while we visited with Laura and Jay Moore who live at

601 Amarillo, my grandparent's former home.

This inside of the Moore home flooded me with memories of good times spent in Abilene for the past eighty years. "Mammam" was always a generous host to me, Bryan and Tom when we visited with our parents. Here, in my great-grandmother's home. I felt welcomed and joyful.

From the time that the wheels of our plane touched the tarmac to when we took off again, Stan Trammell was a charming research companion and tour guide. It was splendid to look across the table into the dark brown Trammell eyes of my cousin. Stan made me feel quite at home, again, in West Texas.

There were three definite locations in West Texas that have particular history for the Trammell clan: Abilene, Hamlin, and Sweetwater. After visiting at the Moore's home we went to the Abilene Municipal Cemetery to visit our loved ones

Sue Trammell Whitfield and Stan Trammell at 601 Amarillo.

Stan Trammell about six years old on the Sims Ranch

Katie Sue Reid and Frank Phillip Trammell.

The 1910 separation of Walter Trammell and Fay Young was not amicable, and they rarely if ever spoke again. The second marriage of my grandfather Walter was to Sallie Sims. This union produced a son Frank Phillip (left) born in 1917. At the time of his birth, Tex and Aunt Mary were teenagers and delighted to have a step-brother.

When he reached adulthood, Frank laid eyes on Katie Sue Reid at Tom's Ice Cream shop in Sweetwater. Family members remarked that it was 'love at first sight'. A short time later they married on Christmas Eve in 1940. Their son, Stan grew up frequenting the Sims Ranch where Walter and Sallie lived. My father Tex spent time at both the Sims and the Y6 Ranch. When Stan attended college in Abilene he spent a lot of time with Aunt Mary. She took him under his wing, much to the dismay of her mother, Fay. Because of the strong Trammell family resemblance, it took Fay a while to adjust to having Stan as a guest in her home. Aunt Mary was persistent and eventually "Mammam" got past her reluctance to accept Walter and Sallie's grandson.

Stan recently told me, "Aunt Mary was the most gregarious, generous, caring and humble person. When she opened a school for single mothers in Abilene, they wanted to do a lot of publicity but would not agree. She wanted to help, but did not want the limelight. She had a heart as big as Texas for people and animals in need."

Abilene Municipal Cemetery and graves sites of Mary Jane Trammell and Fay Young Morton.

Fay Young Morton (1881- 1969)

Fay Morton "Mammam" was a beauty who took very good care of her creamy skin. By contrast, her daughter Mary was an outdoorswoman, often sporting a well-earned tan. When Fay's husband Barney Morton died suddenly in 1929, she moved to Abilene and eventually to the Y6 ranch in Hamlin. Despite having lived at the Rice Hotel for almost fifteen years, "Mammam" adapted back to ranch life with the same vigor and focus as when she played bridge. She evolved from a ranch owner to a stockman to a breeder. Her Herefords were known and admired throughout Jones and Navarro Counties. She turned the ranch house from a rustic abode to a lovely residence with china and antiques. Her refinement was esteemed among all who knew her, including me.

Samuel Cook Young (1848- 1928)

Here is a later picture of my great grandparents

Fay's parents Sam Cook Young and Julia 'Jennie" Bryan Young were married on April 7, 1880. He was 31, and although she was only 17 years old, it was a true love story. They lived in harmony until his death in 1928 at their residence at 601 Amarillo in Abilene. After his passing, the broken hearted Julia "Jennie" Bryan was known to only dress in black until her death in 1947. Their home was the location of many wedding and engagement luncheons, debutante teas and baptism brunches. They had a large extended family that included the Legett and Jones cousins. It was Sam and Julia's estate that left their only child Fay Morton the Y6 ranch in Hamlin, Texas. Aunt Mary was only fifteen when Grandfather Young died, Aunt Mary spent many hours in Sam and Jennie's company during her years in Abilene and Hamlin. I remember great-grandmother Young as a delightful woman, wonderfully creative with handicrafts and a fantastic story teller. We spent hours on the Y6 porch being entertained by her ghost stories. Perhaps she was the origin of Aunt Mary's oratory talent.

Julia Jennie Young Bryan (1862- 1947)

Sam and Jennie had a second child eight years after the birth of my grandmother, Fay. Lora Legett Young lived only eighteen days. Jennie was only twenty-six years of age and there is no record of the reason for Lora's illness. Childhood diseases such as cholera and diphtheria were commonplace and infant mortality was high. The Youngs did not have any more children and Fay would say that she was brought up as a pet. A lovely one in my opinion!

Wyres Obelisk at Abilene Municipal Cemetery

Headstone of Robert Wyres

In the Abilene Municipal Cemetery, my great-great-great grandfather Robert Wyres' resting place is marked with an obelisk. The *obelisk* is an Egyptian motif that *represents* a ray of light or symbol of ascension, with its pyramidal point directed to Heaven. This one has a single sentiment written at the base the word "GONE". He moved his family to St. Augustine, Texas from Virginia just in time for his first born son Victor in 1835. My great-great- grandmother Sophia was born two years later while Texas was still a republic.

We drove the short Jaunt from Abeline to Hamlin, and the Y6 ranch

In 1950 Fay Young Morton "Mammam" surveys her holdings during a day trip 'drive around' the ranch. I was with her on this trip and was happy that she agreed to pose for this picture.

Fay Young Morton sitting on porch of the bunk house. After oil was discovered beneath the ranch land, "Mammam" made many exterior and interior improvements. The clapboard houses were stylized with rock found on the land.

The Y6 Ranch bunk house where the cowboys stayed is now used as a guest house today in 2014.

This is a panoramic view of the stables shortly after "Mammam" completed renovations and used rock from the Y6 for siding.

The Y6 Ranch house today where the Martha M. Ferguson entertains her friends and family.

"Aunt Mary was her own person...unchallenged, undaunted and unchanged by the popular trend or by the opinion her peers or by the demands of society. I loved her so much".

Martha M. Ferguson, owner the Y6 Ranch, Hamlin, Texas.

"Mammam" at the BBQ pit where cowboys, friends, and relatives spent nights spinning folktales.

The stationery masthead of a bull and rope (above) was designed by my grandmother Fay. We were delighted to meet with Martha Ferguson, current owner of the Y6 Ranch, and tour this home which meant so much to me and my family. She kept many of the details that Fay and Aunt Mary had added to the decor. The stone fireplace, bedroom fireplace bathroom, towels, and tile were original to the home I knew.

Bryan, Tom, and our father Tex as they looked when we were on vacation. Dad wore khaki pants and shirt with cowboy boots for leisure activities. While at the Y6 Ranch we spent time learning how to ride horses and shoot targets.

"Mammam" raised prize winning Hereford cattle.

The Y6 in Hamlin, Texas 2014. There had been a good amount of rainfall and it was green and picturesque.

On the road to Sweetwater, Texas

The next morning we left Abilene and drove less than an hour to Sweetwater, Texas. We took the same road that family members have traveled for almost two hundred years. The Wyres family by horse, the Trammell's by buggy, the Young's by train and the rest of us by cars. We were in Texas by 1837 with the birth in St. Augustine of my great-great grandmother Sophia Wyres. The Trammell's arrived in Sweetwater in the early 1880's when Thomas Trammell and Mary Jane Newman settled in this small town. In 1881, traveling at full speed by wagon would have taken seven hours between Abilene and Sweetwater.   Around this same year, my maternal great-grandparents, Sam and Jennie Young were standing on a train's caboose with baby Fay in their arms as they arrived in Abilene. One hundred thirty three years of Trammell history rests in this arid West Texas land.

Market day in Sweetwater where farmers wait with their wagons to unload cotton bales and other supplies for shipment by train.

Local entertainment in Sweetwater. The circus came through at least twice a year and drew a large crowd of curious cowboys stopping to watch the camels and elephants. Notice a large crowd of women have all gathered on the porch of the mercantile post while the men with their wagons line the street.

The Sweetwater Post Office was perched on rocks to lift it off the ground for protection during a "norther". The buildings contents inside of letters and packages needed protection from elements which seeped through clapboard siding. By this time of this photograph, the United States Postal service was 110 years old, but Texas still had pony express riders from April 1860 to October 1861.

"St. Joseph (Missouri) was the starting point for the nearly 2,000-mile central route to the West. Except for a few forts and settlements, the route beyond St. Joseph was a vast, unknown land, inhabited primarily by Native Americans" U.S. Postal Service

Sweetwater Cemetery

My great-grandfather Thomas Trammell preferred the open range for his cattle. In a "Special Notice" published in the Dallas Weekly Herald on November 15, 1883 he and other fourteen stockmen from Nolan and Fisher criticized barb wire. *"Barbed wire fences should be condemned as unfit for the uses they are intended or else make the owner responsible for the damages they do. The manner in which these fences are usually built gives no warning until you dash onto what cannot be seen risking life and horse and it not infrequently occurs that both rider a horse are maimed for life."* Thomas Trammell is called the "Father of Sweetwater."

Sweetwater Cemetery Trammell Plot (2014)

Thomas Trammell (1848-1919)

My great-great-grandfather, Martin Newman, was involved in the farming and stock business. His wife, Miss Elizabeth Polk of Tennessee was a distant relative of President James K. Polk. The Newman family moved to Texas from Arkansas around 1850 settling in Navarro County. Mary Jane was seventeen when Thomas Trammell asked for her hand in marriage. They remained in Navarro County for nine years living with the Newman family. Having had the opportunity to save up money, they moved with their three small sons out of the Newman home and within two years planted roots in Sweetwater where they lived the remainder of the lives.

Mary Jane Newman and friends on a Sunday horse ride through Sweetwater. Courtesy of the Pioneer City County Museum in Sweetwater.

Fifty-three-year-old Thomas Trammell smiles from the front of his new home. He was married to Mary Jane Newman in 1872 and waited twenty-eight years to build such a beautiful place. Unfortunately Mary Jane was only able to enjoy this new house for five years as she died on February 24, 1906.

Sweetwater Cemetery in Nolan County

Mary graduated from Rice Institute in 1926 and moved to Abilene. From 1928 to 1940 she worked as a copywriter solicitor at the *Abilene Reporter News*, where her salary was $225 a month. In 1940 she returned to Houston, where she held the same position for one year at the *Houston Post* and the following year at their competitor, the *Houston Chronicle*. Her boss at the *Post* was none other than Oveta Culp Hobby, while at the *Chronicle* she worked under Maurice Bright. These jobs in Houston paid less than Abilene and her salary was just $150 a month. Today, that would be around $2,496.95.

By 1935 she would frequent the Y6 ranch where her mother Fay was fastidiously making a go of the ranching business. The *Abilene Reporter* on May 4, 1939 noted Mary Jane, her mother Fay Young Morton, and their ranch foreman Bob Kroger as attending the opening of the Abilene Agricultural Building, *"Right alongside her (Fay Young Morton) through the days tour rode her daughter and ranch foreman. Moving bag and baggage from their Abilene home to their re-done ranch home on their 9,000-acre Y6 Ranch, which spills over from Jones into Stonewall County, the mother and daughter team is devoting their time to the raising of Hereford cattle."*

Y6 Ranch letterhead designed by Fay "Mammam" Morton

At the outbreak of World War II, Mary Jane answered the nation's need for womanpower and went to Corpus Christi to work at the new Navy Air Base as a civil servant in the Assembly and Repair Department. If you can imagine a bandana on her head and sleeves rolled up, attending to the drilling of screws on a plane's wing, that image would not be far off. She began in 1942 as a Helper Metalsmith at $5 a day and by 1947 she had been promoted to Aviation Metalsmith with a daily salary of $13.28. The Corpus Christi facility where she worked was established in 1941 to meet the needs of the war effort in the skies over Germany and Japan.

Naval Aircraft Factory 1942

The base covered twenty thousand acres and had eight hundred instructors taking in classes of three hundred new cadets every month. Completed only three months below the Japanese attack on Pearl Harbor, the base was a crucial source for planes and aviators. It is not known whether Aunt Mary knew a young cadet who later was elected President of the United States, George H.W. Bush. He graduated from this Naval Air Base in 1943, AT 19, he was the youngest pilot on record. At the end of her civilian service, Mary returned to Abilene where she and her mother enriched the holdings of the Y6 Ranch.

Aunt Mary and "Mammam" on vacation in Italy.

I can't remember "Mammam " ever talking aloud about Sweetwater or her first husband, Walter. Her trips to Sweetwater were very rare, but Aunt Mary, Tex and our family went several times as I can remember. When we received the phone call that my grandfather Walter had passed away, I remember we, immediately jumped in the car for the six hour drive to Sweetwater.

With homes in both Hamlin and Abilene, Aunt Mary and "Mammam" lived a nice existence. They found great pleasure in travel and went around the world at least once. The picture to the left is Aunt Mary and Fay in Italy.

Vic Behrens was my friend and escort to the dance in Abilene.

When I was eighteen, in 1951, my family traveled to the Cotillion Christmas Dance at the Abilene Country Club. Although we lived in Houston, Mammam made sure to invite local children spend time and befriend us, so I knew many of other girls. *The Abilene Reporter Newspaper* described our Christmas Cotillion Ball in great detail-

"Sue Trammell, the only daughter of Mr. and Mrs. W. B. Trammell, and the only granddaughter of Mrs. Fay Young Morton of the Y6 Ranch, Hamlin... Traditions and color of Cotillion Club's previous Christmas Belle presentations were repeated as five coeds were introduced as 1951 Belle's at the Club's annual Christmas Week Party at the Abilene Country Club... The Belles all wore white bouffant and strapless models with gilt ornamentation, long white gloves and each carried a cascade bouquet of red Better Times rosebud...Miss Trammell wore nylon net with crinoline petticoats. The frock was inset with panels of silver lace embroidered with silver. The draped bodice with outlined with rhinestone butterflies. Her escort was Vic Behrens Jr. Mrs. Fay Young Morton was gowned in charcoal gray faille – taffeta stole collar fashion inset with heavy embroidery in matching color. Her daughter Mary Jane Trammell wore a Dior original in blue taffeta, with bodice embroidered with sequins. Jacketed in taffeta, the costume was a modified-hoop model... Mrs. W. B. Trammell of Houston wore a strapless, demitasse length beige lace dress, with lace design defined with iridescent. She wore satin slippers and long gloves in matching color."

At the Abilene Country Club chandeliers cast an essence of elegance across the dance floor. The night of my debut the room was filled with gorgeous flowers. Aunt Mary dressed in a Dior original which proved her devotion to me as this was not a regular style of dress for her. She was much more comfortable in slacks.

The Abilene Country Club today, where sixty three years ago I danced at my debut. This room is still as beautiful as it was the night of the Christmas Cottilion Ball.

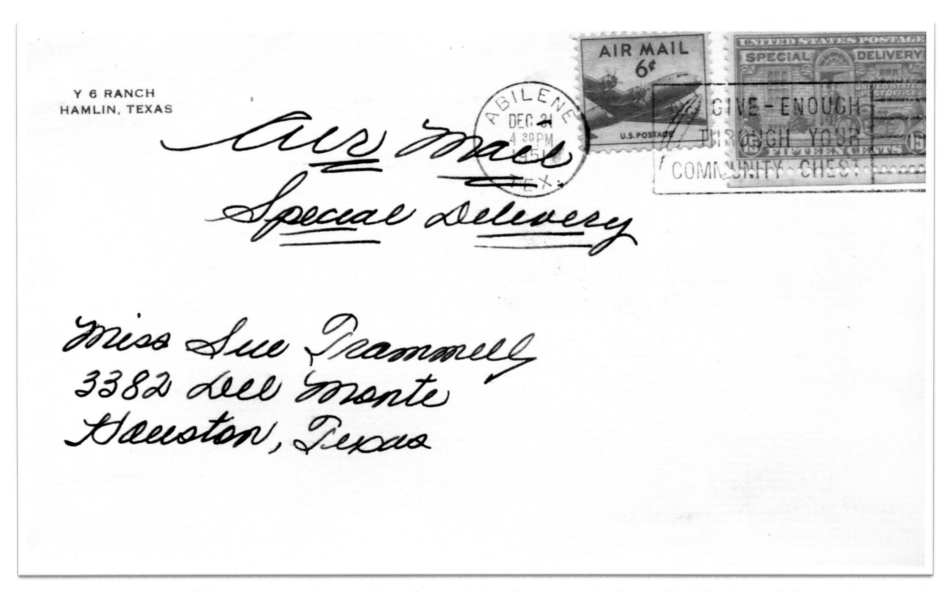

Aunt Mary was a wonderful letter writer and storyteller. After my debut she sent me this letter which I've kept safe for sixty four years. I felt sharing her own words would best illustrate her views on life and justice.

Y6 Ranch
HAMLIN, TEXAS

Monday-
Last day 1951

my precious Sue.
your conquest of this arid country is complete. you took it in your stride with your beauty, grace, poise & charm. you are truly the 'Toast' of every gathering. your grandmother & old maid aunt have no modesty- our pride knows no bounds. We frankly admit our little girl is quite the loveliest ever to take a social bow.
To see 'our Belle' of today its hard to remember a Yuletide 18 years ago. Little hope did we have of her precious life much less a triumphant social campaign any where- any time. To God, to science, to nature & a well heeled pocket book we are humbly grateful

Her handwriting slants to the right which demonstrates an exuberant personality. The weight of her pen stroke signifies a purposeful message, I always say that
"He broke the mold when God made Aunt Mary."

Monday-
Last day 1951
My precious Sue:
Your conquest of this arid country is complete. You took it in your stride with your beauty, grace, poise, & charm. You are truly the 'Toast' of every gathering. Your grandmother & old maid aunt have no modesty-our pride knows no bounds. We frankly admit our little girl is quite the loveliest ever to take a social bow. To see 'our Belle' of today it's hard to remember a yuletide 18 years ago. Little hope did we have of her precious life much less a triumphant social campaign anywhere-any time. To God, to science, to nature & a well healed pocket book we are humbly grateful. So grateful we don't want to forget our great blessing or lose sight of those where youth, beauty &radiance are shackled to a wheel chair. Joan Byram's little face has haunted me since we walked in Myrtle's living room. She would have stood with you had it not been for a rigid back & useless legs. Fate was cruel to her but precious one, let's extend some deed, some gesture of kindness that will lighten her burden & give her a small respite from the dull existence she must endure. The greatest happiness & pleasure I've had in life is doing favors & small services for others. The Boy Scout Creed & the Golden Rule are truly the principles to live by. This sounds like a broadcast from a pulpit-I don't mean to preach—I do want one thing—it is my sole motive. To cram into your promising life all of the joy and happiness possible & to have your profit by my 50 years of blundering & stumbling along. how a letter from you would mean much to Joan-so let's take time out and & tell her- you enjoyed seeing her at Myrtles & were sorry you didn't get to drop by or have her down to the hotel on your flying sojourn & that come summer or your next trip you hope to get together with her & have a real old fashioned 'gab fest'! Also tell her your brother Bryan would like another chance to date Dale but he'd like a little advance notice & enough health to keep the engagement. Our stock hit a new low with the Byrams & only you can raise it. Lettie Fawcett, society ed. Reporter told me yesterday that she had known every member of this family intimately & that you are the loveliest-most beautiful of five generations & a perfect successor to the once 'Queen of Love & Beauty' that stormed West Texas in the early 1900's. Only I don't want you to turn out with some of her characteristics—Thoughtfulness, consideration, love of fellow-man & loyalty are the greatest attributes any human being can possess- you have these traits Sue. Plus a perfect body & a fine mind. Cultivate and nourish them. The payoff is greater than all of life's dividends. Thanks again for coming out. It was, as I say, one of life's biggest & most pleasant moments for me and Ma Mam. It will ever be a vivid pleasant treasure n my store house of memories.   With all my heart I love you – Your Aunt Mary"

Bryan, Fay "Mammam" Morton and Thomas dressed to the hilt. She was never happier than in the company of her handsome grandsons. I have such wonderful memories of visiting West Texas.

Aunt Mary, "Mammam" and Anita Patterson on one of their many adventures. Anita was an Abilene travel agent who planned our family vacations. The Fondrens and Trammells traveled together often and memories from these trips are priceless.

Excerpt from *Common Sense*, written in 1776 by Thomas Paine which Aunt Mary hung on her wall. She gave a printed and framed copy of this creed to several individuals including Martha Ferguson and Stan Trammell. The only difference is that she changed the very last word from Entrepreneur to American.

"I do not choose to be a common man.
It is my right to be uncommon … if I can.
I seek opportunity … not security.
I do not wish to be a kept citizen,
Humbled and dulled by having the State look after me.
I want to take the calculated risk,
To dream and to build. To fail and to succeed.
I refuse to barter incentive for a dole;
I prefer the challenges of life to the guaranteed existence;
The thrill of fulfillment to the stale calm of Utopia.
I will not trade freedom for beneficence
Nor my dignity for a handout
I will never cower before any master
Nor bend to any threat.
It is my heritage to stand erect, proud and unafraid;
To think and act for myself,
To enjoy the benefit of my creations
And to face the world boldly and say:
This, with God's help, I have done.
All this is what it means to be an" AMERICAN.

"Mary was every child's "Fairy Godmother" and she made children of all ages feel loved, special and important. Her home was always open to youth and teenagers, who loved to be with Mary and to listen to her stories of all of the fun times she had experienced throughout her life. She was a special "matchmaker," who always had the perfect out of town escort in mind for any of Abilene's Cotillion Belles; she introduced the couple and was happy to host the young gentleman as her houseguest for all of the parties. She was always ready to entertain, on a moment's notice, by rolling up her rugs and cranking up the Victrola for impromptu parties for the teenagers. Everyone loved Mary!"

Martha Minter Ferguson

"Aunt Mary had a heart as big as Texas. She loved people, being around them, and she loved to help people even if they were strangers. She loved to whistle to any tune on the record player or radio. In college I had a mustang and it took Aunt Mary forever to get in it. She liked to feel like she was young again. We'd put all the windows down and drive fast and she would whistle, whistle all the way. She was so smart. If she helped me with an assignment, I always got a great grade. She was a patient teacher. She knew world history, Abilene history, West Texas history, and Hamlin. She loved all history. Aunt Mary was a big influence on me during my college days. She was full of life and fun."

Stan Trammell

I can only remember my grandfather Walter Trammell in Houston twice. This picture was taken in 1945 (Left to right) my mother 'Sweetie', Grandfather, Aunt Mary, and Dad holding my brother Tom. Bryan and I are standing in front. It was a fun Trammell reunion.